D0952242

Praise for *WE*

"In a hypercompetitive business environment, gender parity is essential to success. Rania Anderson delivers the evidence-based framework for frontline managers to senior executives who are serious about improving the workplace through a commitment to action and rewriting the gender playbook. Gender partnerships that leverage the collective strengths of men and women will be the hallmark of the modern workplace designed for economic prosperity. By taking action together, WE can succeed in creating an equitable workplace where everyone wins."

–David G. Smith, PhD, Associate Professor of Sociology, National Security Affairs Department, United States Naval War College, coauthor of *Athena Rising: How and Why Men Should Mentor Women*

"This book is a must-read for all male leaders looking for guidance on how to work more effectively with women. *WE* sheds light on what to DO versus what not to do. Leveraging her deep experience as an executive business coach, Rania Anderson shares intentional, proactive, and research-based actions to retain and advance women in the workplace."

–Jeffery Tobias Halter, President of YWomen, corporate gender strategist, author, thought leader

"One of the classic challenges in gender equality work is engaging men. In this book, Rania Anderson provides a concrete plan for how to take it to the next level – WE 4.0 offers men a vision of why and how they must get onboard and contribute to gender equality in ways that make the work all of us do count for even more. Engagement at the top has always been important, but this book shows us how to create engagement throughout an entire organization. I'll definitely be recommending this to organizations that know they need to change – and to those that don't!"

–Curt Rice, PhD, Leader of Norway's Committee on Gender Balance and Diversity in Research and President, Oslo Metropolitan University

"For entrepreneurs, finding the right talent is a significant challenge, especially in the gritty early years. That's precisely why startup founders – 65% of whom are male – can't afford to overlook the insights and contributions that women will make to the growth of their firms. Rania Anderson provides a compelling, well-timed roadmap for entrepreneurs to leverage the strengths of a gender-diverse team, work effectively together, and produce better outcomes for everyone."

–Wendy Guillies, President and CEO,
Ewing Marion Kauffman Foundation

"The majority of leaders are men. They can drive change on gender equality. I have studied men in senior leadership and middle-management positions to find out how men can create gender-inclusive environments. Anderson drills down into these practices and provides the reader with a playbook guiding what to specifically say and do, so that men and managers can no longer claim they don't know what to do!"

–Elisabeth Kelan, PhD, Professor of Leadership,
Cranfield School of Management

"Rania Anderson's WE quite rightly challenges the pervasive and damaging 'myth of meritocracy.' She argues that men need to be more reflective and take action to change their work environment. As she points out, only then can we get closer to a truly level playing field."

–Adam Quinton, Founder/CEO of Lucas Point Ventures and Adjunct
Professor at the Columbia University School of International
and Public Affairs

"I have always said that women don't need men to stand up for them; women need men to stand beside them in the battle against inequality. I'm really glad there is now a book that highlights key business cases for individuals and organizations to learn from."

–Khalid Alkhudair, social entrepreneur, Founder and CEO of Glowork,
an employment organization for women in Saudi Arabia

WE

WE

MEN, WOMEN, AND THE DECISIVE FORMULA FOR WINNING AT WORK

RANIA H. ANDERSON

WILEY

Library of Congress Cataloging-in-Publication Data

Names: Anderson, Rania H., 1961- author.
Title: We : men, women, and the decisive formula for winning at work / Rania H. Anderson.
Description: Hoboken, NJ : John Wiley & Sons, Inc., [2019] | Includes bibliographical references and index. |
Identifiers: LCCN 2018032755 (print) | LCCN 2018034801 (ebook) | ISBN 9781119524663 (Adobe PDF) | ISBN 9781119524700 (ePub) | ISBN 9781119524694 (hardcover)
Subjects: LCSH: Sex role in the work environment. | Sex discrimination in employment–Prevention. | Diversity in the workplace. | Success in business.
Classification: LCC HD6060.6 (ebook) | LCC HD6060.6 .A53 2019 (print) | DDC 658.4/09–dc23
LC record available at https://lccn.loc.gov/2018032755

Printed in the United States of America.

V10003773_082318

For the two men who support me the most,
my husband, Lance, and my son, Nick.
And for my Dad, my first male champion.

Contents

2 The WE 4.0 Framework   54

Four actions that maximize your own success and business results when men and women work equally together. How you can individually effect change where you are now regardless of what's happening around you.

3 Eliminate   66

What to stop. Horror stories, hero stories, and techniques the savviest leaders use. Specific ways to interrupt unconscious bias and improve your work environment so that everyone has an equal opportunity to succeed.

4 Expand   92

What to increase. How you can recruit, retain, give direct feedback, and network with women. Be a sponsor, not just a mentor. Develop female talent and improve your own results.

5 Encourage   128

How to support. Discover what most men and managers miss in meetings and what to do about it. Take simple steps to make women and their contributions more visible. Unlock opportunities for yourself, women, and your company through your support and encouragement.

6 Engage   152

How to participate. Leave "loudly," get in on "work-keeping," and learn the secrets of leaders who transform work environments and champion equality. Be the example. This isn't your father's workplace.

Conclusion 167

WE 4.0 at a Glance 174

WE 4.0 Checklist 178

Foreword

Dominic Barton, Global Managing Partner,
McKinsey & Company

The two most important words in Rania H. Anderson's indispensable book are "you" and "specific."

The "you" is any leader – but perhaps especially men – who works with or supervises women. This is not a book about what *institutions* should do to become more inclusive and diverse. It is about what *you* can do to make your workplace more inclusive and diverse – and, in the process, more effective, more profitable, and more successful.

That's important, because it's up to *you* to take the steps needed to ensure gender parity in your workplace. Your heart may have been in the right place for years, and you may well regard yourself as an enlightened manager. But are your top jobs occupied disproportionately by men? Are you sponsoring women the way you sponsor men? Are women commanding equal salaries? Good intentions don't matter. Actions do.

I am the first to admit that leading change in this area can be challenging, and progress can be maddeningly slow even when an organization does all the right things. That said, the sad fact is that many managers have been too slow to even try to maximize the potential of what Anderson aptly calls "the most underutilized asset the world has" – women.

At a moment when companies are turning themselves inside out to become more agile and innovative, can you really afford to reward old behaviors that stymie half of your potential workforce? When you're constantly surveying the horizon for new competitors, can you really afford to sideline people whose experiences can expand your vision? When women control $20 trillion of purchasing power, when they drive 70–85% of all consumer purchasing decisions and even buy more cars and consumer electronics than men, can you afford to sit by as your company's women fail to rise to leadership roles? The answer to each question, of course, is "No." As Anderson puts it, "Just as we can calculate a return on equity, we can also calculate a return on equality."

As a business leader, you have the opportunity to change your workplace every day, and this should be your playbook.

That's where the book's other critical word – "specific" – comes into play. Many well-intentioned leaders simply don't know how to drive gender parity. You may not be sure how to begin the process of changing the nature of your workplace so that women have the same opportunities as men. That may seem like such a daunting task.

The specifics in this book demystify the process. Anderson does this in many ways. She explains with great precision the research on what women want from their work and workplace. She creates a framework, called *WE 4.0*, for how women and men can work equally, share leadership, and succeed together. She gives you a vocabulary and questions to ask to examine your existing practices for signs of unconscious bias. Most importantly, she describes the actions needed at the individual level to build diverse, high-performing teams and equitable work environments. Each chapter includes an invaluable self-assessment checklist, a set of tasks to get you started, and examples from people who have tackled this problem in their own workplaces.

Anderson's examples are drawn from her extensive work helping leaders around the world with their efforts to create workplaces where women can thrive. The examples are unique and yet relatable, like the

Jordanian investor who stands out by backing companies run by Arab women; the GE leader who sponsors a female employee by throwing the most critical tasks her way; or the one woman in a four-partner group who finally insisted that the men share in the administrative tasks they kept unconsciously passing off onto her. I found that many of her examples highlighted complicated work scenarios similar to ones I have encountered during my own career, and I'm sure you will as well.

Gender equity has been increasing on the agenda of many companies over the past several years, thanks in part to women (and some men) calling out the biases – and sometimes egregious behaviors – that have prevented many women from reaching their full potential. This book takes what too many leaders see as an intractable challenge and provides clear, step-by-step recommendations on how to address the underlying issues.

I hope that Anderson's readers will lead the process of truly changing our workplaces into gender-equal environments. Sure, it's time, and sure, it's the right thing to do. But as someone who regularly engages with the CEOs of the world's most valuable companies, I see the real cost of the status quo: an enormous waste of economic, intellectual, and innovative potential.

Put simply, you cannot win without a workplace where women and men have equal opportunities, equal input, and equal power. Anderson points out that creating such a workplace is a broader, more ambitious goal than creating a workplace where women "fit in." But true gender equality is the goal we should all be striving for. In a world where women represent 50% or more of the outstanding talent, anything less is an abdication of your fiduciary responsibility.

Rania Anderson's remarkably lucid book is a subtle gem. It is so straightforward, so honest, and, yes, so specific. The subject it tackles is enormous, global, and complicated. And yet, when I read this slender volume, the truly equitable workplace seems more of a possibility than ever, a vision within reach rather than an impossible dream. It's a vision that won't come to be without your active leadership and participation. Cracking open this book was a great first step. Good luck with the rest of the journey. With Rania Anderson as your guide, I'm sure it will be illuminating, productive, inspiring and, ultimately, profitable.

June 14, 2018

Introduction

Would you turn down an idea to build a brand in a few years that results in more than $200 million in revenue? What if you could hire someone who doubled, tripled, or even improved your results ten-fold? If there was a simple way to increase your market share, would you take it? What if you knew that a coworker, whom you largely ignore, knew something that would contribute to your rapid promotion to senior vice president? Would you pay attention?

These are real circumstances in which men found themselves. The smart and savvy ones saw the opportunity and grabbed it by listening, hiring, or working well with a woman.

You are one of these men. You're one of the good guys. You don't enjoy succeeding at someone else's expense. You are committed to fair play. You want to do the right things related to women in the workplace. You know you do. You see what's going on in some companies. No one needs to explain how wrong it is to you. You are fed up. You are not part of the "bro culture." You are embarrassed by the actions of some presidents, CEOs, and venture capitalists (VCs). You don't want to be identified with them, or turn a blind eye any longer. Your wife, sister, mother, and/or daughter work, and they've told you about the difficult circumstances with which women deal in the workplace, and you don't approve. You also want what's best for your son. You want to be happier at work.

You respect women and know their value. You are well aware of the business case for why the presence of more women in the workforce, particularly in leadership roles, will help you, your company, and your family. You have and see job openings that are hard to fill. You know that more than 50% of university graduates globally are women. You see the war for talent that's underway to attract and retain the brightest minds and the people with the best skills. You know that many of the brightest minds are women: Mary Barra, Chairman and CEO of General Motors; Sheryl Sandberg, COO of Facebook; Indra Nooyi, CEO of PepsiCo; Safra Catz, co-CEO of Oracle; and Raja Easa Al Gurg, Managing Director, Easa Saleh Al Gurg Group are a few examples. Think of the women you know, the women you work with and see regularly. Your highly talented coworker may be sitting in the cubicle right next to yours.

You are ambitious, and you care about your career. You want to win. You are not afraid that you will lose your job or miss out on a promotion you deserve if women are treated equitably. You cherish competition – bring it on! Competing against top performers elevates your game. You've never believed that there are a finite number of jobs or opportunities. Innovation and new job creation is all around you. And who wouldn't want some of the women I just named on their team or leading them? Successful women leaders hire, develop, and advance men's careers and businesses all over the world. Talent – in no matter which gender it appears – rewards those who leverage it.

You are doing your best. You are tired of being told that you have unconscious bias – and of course, everyone does! You recognize that more diversity will benefit everyone, not just the groups of people who were previously left out or discriminated against.

Furthermore, you don't subscribe to outdated cultural/societal views of the role of women. You consider your wife/girlfriend as your partner, not your housekeeper, and you share household tasks and childcare duties with her. You enjoy life outside of work: being with your family, your children (if you have them), and your friends. You want the women you work with and love to have work environments that are free of bias or discrimination and full of opportunity. You want your son to have all the career options he'd like to consider.

You want to do the right thing in your workplace and in society. But you don't know how to change what's been happening or make things better. You are afraid of saying or doing the wrong things, and you don't want to be afraid anymore. While you understand how the #MeToo outpouring occurred and admire the courage of women who came forward, you may also be worried and even a little anxious. You are worried about what the post-#MeToo work environment means for solid, professional relationships between men and women at work. You have female colleagues and clients and don't want your interactions with them to be strained. Will it still be possible to make a female friend at work? Are the days of meeting a future girlfriend or wife at work gone forever? And you are fearful because men and women can let private conversations sometimes go to places that later cause regret and harm. Who hasn't made this mistake?

You'd like to know more about how increasing gender diversity can specifically help you with your own career or business aspirations and not lead to fewer opportunities for you, other men, and your son. If you just knew what it all meant and what to do about it in simple, straightforward, actionable and pragmatic terms.

Over 50 percent of business leaders said they need to do more to attract, retain, and promote women to leadership positions.[1]

–Ernst & Young Global Limited

Four Guiding Truths

I have worked with, coached, and developed male and female business leaders for the past 25 years. I've worked with them in the United States, Latin America, Eastern Europe, the Middle East, South Africa, and Australia. I've worked with them one-on-one and in groups. I've also surveyed and interviewed them. Here's what I've observed:

1. Most men in professional settings are focused on their own careers. They want to win and to be a part of winning teams. They have no interest in keeping women down.

2. Like men, most women in professional settings are focused on their own careers. They want to be members of high-performing teams to solve problems and win in the marketplace. They don't think that men are intentionally boxing them out.

3. *Both* men and women unconsciously and consciously thwart the efforts and advancements of women.

4. Women don't want to walk behind men or in front of them. They want to walk beside them. They know, like you know, that the world's problems and opportunities can only be solved through the shared engagement and leadership of men and women – a vision of workplace gender parity that I term *WE 4.0*.

Over the past decade, I've focused much of my attention largely on equipping women around the world to accelerate their business success. During this period, I wrote *Undeterred: The Six Success Habits of Women in Emerging Economies,* the first career-advice book for women in these markets, and I spoke to thousands of women at conferences, universities, and corporations. I've guided women on what to do and say to achieve their personal definition of professional or business success and on how to work more effectively with men.

I didn't choose to do this work to "help" women. I don't think about it that way. Women don't need my help, as they are capable on their own. What drives me is global economic advancement. I believe that educated women are the most underutilized asset the world has and that we will drive economic prosperity when men and women work together as equals. I wanted to use my background and expertise to increase the economic participation and leadership of women and to equip men and managers to leverage the collective strengths of both men and women. So, that's what I set out to do.

To address the needs that professional women and female entrepreneurs expressed to me, and based on my research findings, I launched The Way WoMen

Work, initially a career-advice website for women in emerging economies. Today, the platform serves a much broader audience and now also provides men, managers, and leaders with actions that improve their results by working more effectively with women.

I've spoken to thousands of women around the world at companies, conferences, and universities sharing concrete, research-based actionable advice that they could immediately implement to make a difference in their careers and businesses. Women regularly write to tell me about their pay raises and promotions. Trupti Jain, an entrepreneur I coached as part of the Cartier Women's Initiative, received an award of USD $100,000. The company she cofounded with her husband is transforming agricultural irrigation.

Often when women follow up with me to talk about their improved success, they also talk about improved relationships with male colleagues and bosses, and, very importantly to them, with their husbands.

Female talent remains one of the most underutilized business resources, either squandered through lack of progression or untapped from the onset.[2]

–*World Economic Forum*

I was pleased and gratified by the impact I was making, and I wasn't looking to change direction until I was confronted head-on by an urgent need in the marketplace, and three opportunities converged right in front of me compelling me to write this book.

Men began asking me to help them work more effectively with women. As I walked down the hallways of leading companies around the world, men literally stopped me to tell me something like this: "Why are people like you always here to speak to, or train women? It's as if something is wrong with women such that they must keep going through remedial training. How come no one ever comes to train us on how to improve the way we work with women? I already understand the business case for why we need more women. I acutely feel the need for high-performing talent. What I need is someone to tell me how to do a better job recruiting and retaining women."

Dominic Barton, the global managing director of McKinsey & Company, framed it like this: "Front-line managers need help. Change does not happen without the full engagement of front-line leaders. These are the plant managers, regional sales leaders, store managers, team coaches, and general managers who make companies tick."[3]

A senior male leader at a public entity led by a female CEO whose company, like many other companies, has invested heavily in women's leadership development initiatives, earnestly implored me for help, saying, "We spend a lot of money to develop high-potential women. I want to support the women who have completed our women's leadership development program, but I don't know the best things to do."

On university campuses on four continents, young men in great numbers attended my speaking engagements that were clearly intended for women. On one campus in the Republic of Georgia, the number of male students outnumbered the women in attendance 10 to 1. When I asked the men why they were there, they told me they wanted to know more about working with women because they knew they'd be working with, for, or managing women in their careers. In March 2018, a male university student asked me questions about how I became a "strong" woman. Another question was about how women become "strong" and confident. What makes some women more career-oriented and others not?" Before responding, I inquired why he was asking me these questions. "I want to marry a strong woman. I want a partner in my life." he replied.

These men and their questions captured my attention. When these incidents increased in frequency, I knew

I needed to do something to address their expressed needs. I began with a couple of speaking engagements to small groups of managers, the first of which was at Procter & Gamble in Mexico City. Interest and demand from companies and conference organizers increased. The topic became a major part of my focus and work in the United States, South Africa, Mexico, the UAE, and Ukraine. A few years later, and after making positive headway and inroads with managers and leaders, an explosive issue surfaced.

People around the world finally believed that sexual harassment was more frequent and prevalent than they had previously acknowledged. Even though most men are good guys, there are a few bad ones, hogging the spotlight, which cast a pall over other men. To name just a few of the widely reported reprehensible actions of several high-profile leaders that came to light around the time I was writing this book: The United States of America elected a president who spoke openly about groping women. In Silicon Valley, Travis Kalanick, founder of one of the fastest-growing companies in the world, Uber, was forced to resign as CEO of the company. He lost his job in part because he led a workplace culture that condoned making highly inappropriate remarks about women (some by Travis himself), sexual discrimination, and harassment. If that weren't enough, one of Uber's board members,

David Bonderman, made sexist comments at the very meeting the company held to discuss improving its culture. He also was forced to step down.

Then, there was the removal of VCs including Dave McClure as the CEO of 500 Startups, one of the most well-known Silicon Valley business accelerators, after revelations of their sexual misconduct. Around the same time and adding to the mountains of existing information about prevailing gender inequities, a study was released showing that VCs – *both* male *and* female VCs – ask women entrepreneurs different types of questions than they ask male entrepreneurs when they consider pitches for funding. They tend to ask men questions about the potential for gains (the upside) and women about the potential for losses (the downside).[4] Dana Kanze at Columbia University, one of the people who conducted the research, explained to me that asking these types of questions can impact the investor's financial returns by overexposing them to downside risk in investments made in start-ups led by men and underexposing them to the upside risk in start-ups led by women.

In Hollywood and the media sector, the predatory behavior of high-profile men – including Harvey Weinstein, Charlie Rose, Louis CK, and Matt Lauer – was reported on an almost daily basis. The #MeToo movement and its equivalent in many countries took off as thousands of women took to social media, blogs, and mainstream news media outlets to talk how they had been sexually harassed or assaulted. The news media also began to more widely cover harassment of lower-income women who, like some high-profile women, had endured unaddressed hostile work environments for years. In January 2018, the Time's Up movement and fund were launched to support lower-income women seeking justice for sexual harassment and assault in the workplace and to advocate for legislation against companies that tolerate persistent harassment. When the magnitude of the problems that many women face became evident, men and managers felt ill-prepared, confused, and unsure about how to best interact and work effectively with women.

The predominant approaches relied upon to equip and advance women were deemed insufficient to realize the business and economic dividend that would be achieved through gender parity. It became clear that men, managers, and leaders had been largely left out and insufficiently equipped to take individual responsibility to increase female hiring, improve working relationships and work environments for women, and to actively advance them.

McKinsey & Company is globally recognized for its research on closing the gender gap. Here again, from an article written by its managing partner, Dominic Barton, for *The Wall Street Journal*:

"Less than half of all workers see managers taking advantage of the diverse strengths of their teams or considering a diverse lineup of candidates for open positions. What this tells us is that managers are either not getting the message or don't know how to manage differently.

Faced with these challenges, it's time to rewrite our gender playbooks so that they do more to change the fabric of everyday work life by encouraging relentless execution, fresh ideas, and courageous personal actions.

As our research underscores, we need to look more carefully at the day-to-day experiences, for better or worse, of the people in our organizations."[5]

What does all this mean for you?

Gender Parity Is Good for All of Us

Gender equality, men and women working and leading equally together, leads to higher performance and profitability. A plethora of studies show that countries can improve their GDPs if more women participate in the workforce and in leadership roles, that diverse teams are more creative and make better decisions, and that companies with more women in executive roles are more profitable and have higher share prices. Look for more detail about and references to these specific studies in Chapter 1.

Just as important, perhaps more important to you, more working women and women in leadership can improve *your* life and *your* performance. Obviously, gender equality benefits women. But, have you thought about how gender parity also benefits the sons, daughters, and partners of the women?

One study across 24 countries showed that girls raised by a working mother had higher incomes than women whose moms stayed at home full time. And boys raised by working mothers were more likely to contribute to household chores and spend more time caring for family members. "There are very few things, that we know of, that have such a clear effect on gender inequality as being raised by a working mother," says Dr. Kathleen L. McGinn, Professor of Business Administration at Harvard Business School HBS, who conducted the study. "There's a lot of parental guilt about having both parents working outside the home," McGinn says. "But what this research says to us is that not only are you helping your family economically – and helping yourself professionally and emotionally if you have a job you love – but you're also helping your kids. So, I think for both mothers and for fathers, working both inside and outside the home gives your kids a signal that contributions at home and at work are equally valuable, for both men and women. In short, it's good for your kids."[6]

When women have more occupational choices, so do men. When more women work, and are in senior well-paid positions, men don't have to carry the burden of being the sole provider. When more women work, men are more likely to spend more time with their children, which is very positive for both the children and their dads. Almost every single one of the 250 women from around the world whom I interviewed for my book *Undeterred* cited their dad as a major positive influence on their career success.

Gender diversity is also an advantage to you in your career or business. If you are able to build and work effectively with a high-performing diverse team, your results will outpace your peers and your competition. A gender-diverse team is a competitive advantage. It may seem counterintuitive, but when you accelerate the success of women, you accelerate your own success.

Here's my favorite example of how it works. Be sure to read this if you want to get ahead in your career.

Paul, a relationship manager at a bank, didn't spend much time with the female client-service representative on his team. Since his clients were generally pleased with the service they received from her, he didn't give her, or what she did, much thought. As a result, he didn't know much about her, the full range of her capabilities, or her potential until one morning, when he overheard her talking to a client. Without looking at a computer screen or referring to any documents, she rattled off detailed information to the customer about the balances in their accounts. He called her into his office and asked where she was getting the numbers from and how she was able to recount them so easily to the customer. She explained that every morning when she came into the office, she spent time reviewing each client account and relationship and that she had a great memory. He tested her by asking questions about various other client accounts. She was able to correctly answer every one.

Now she had his attention. He asked her why she was in her current role and discovered she'd taken the job because it was the only position available at the time she applied. He asked her about her career interests and ambitions, and she shared that she had higher aspirations and the skills to go along with them. During the conversation, he had an "aha" moment: If they worked closely together, perhaps they both could be much more productive. And if he positioned her to achieve her ambitions, she could help him achieve his.

Paul began to give his coworker more responsibility and stopped assigning small administrative tasks to her as he had formerly done. He spent time with her discussing their clients and strategizing opportunities to further develop their accounts. Their new way of working together resulted in significant growth in their client relationships. Their novel approach was so successful that the bank made a video about the way they worked together as an example and model for similar teams in the bank.

During the next few years, the two of them were assigned and expertly handled the client portfolios of four other teams. They continued to excel. At every opportunity he had, Paul spoke highly about his female colleague to senior leaders and regularly praised and recognized her. She was promoted. He was promoted. Eventually, although they no longer worked together, both he and she became senior vice presidents.

You want to produce results. You want to succeed. You want fair competition and a level playing field. How can you have that if you utilize only half the talent pool and compete with only half the players? This imbalance is what we have in today's work environment.

Progress to Achieve Gender Parity Is Stalled

Globally, we are no longer making strides in our efforts to achieve gender equality. We were told and we believed that when more women were educated and more women joined the workforce, the problem would be solved. But that has not been the case. While the education rate of girls and women around the world has risen and is in many places on parity with the education rates of boys and men, and while entry-level positions in many companies are held equally by men and women, these strides have not translated into significantly more women in leadership, more funding for women entrepreneurs, or more women in executive leadership or as directors on corporate boards. The reality is that the global gender gap actually has widened and that at our current rate of progress, it will take more than two hundred more years to close it![7]

For the past few decades, the primary strategy implemented by institutions to increase gender balance in their workforces and in leadership roles, has been to teach women what they need to do differently: how they can be more confident, how they should ask for a raise, get a sponsor, and improve their personal brands and executive presence. In essence, they train women on what to do to succeed in a "man's world," the business environment where men hold most of the power.

But these institutional and business efforts have largely fallen short. Their approach, on one hand, is to develop women, empower women, and increase the visibility of successful female role models, and on the other hand, to enlist executive leadership commitment and make workplace practices and policies fair and inclusive of the needs of women. While these strategies have been important and necessary inputs to the equation and have brought women to the point of inclusion, they aren't getting us any further.

What is missing? We now recognize that well-intentioned people who work on gender equality, and companies all over the world, have not fully enlisted men and front-line managers and have not equipped them to individually become part of the solution.

Sure, some CEOs and executives have made pledges, set gender-equality goals, and made gender inclusion a priority. Many are deeply dedicated and committed.

The chairman of one of the largest professional services firms in the United States confided in me that some people have even cautioned him not to go "too far" in making changes to increase diversity. And, although many companies and CEOs include gender equality in their top ten business priorities, gender outcomes across the largest companies are not changing.[8]

A central reason for this lack of progress is that middle and front-line managers and male coworkers who interact with women daily have not been looped in. Elisabeth Kelan, PhD, Professor of Leadership at Cranfield School of Management in the United Kingdom, frames the situation like this: "Seventy percent of managers and leaders are men. They are the people who can make change happen."[9]

With the exception of blaming men and telling them that they are unconsciously biased (just like we all are), very little has been done to involve and equip men, and all front-line managers and leaders, to fully include and advance women. Men are told why achieving gender parity is the right thing to do, but you haven't been told why it's right for you and what's in it for you. Most men, managers, and leaders have not made achieving gender balance a business priority. Instead, without personally doing anything about it, they are convinced that with enough time, gender inequality will no longer be an issue. My dad always told me that hope was not a strategy.

The men who stop me in the hallways or raise their hands at the sessions I've conducted for entrepreneurs, managers, and leaders at Fortune 100 companies like P&G, PwC, Barclays, GM, Microsoft, and American Express, are not like the few highly visible, sexist men we read about in the news. They are like you – the managers, entrepreneurs, and coworkers who respect women and want to say and do the right things.

Here's part of the problem. The modern workplace was created by men for men in an era when very few women worked. The intention was not to keep women out. Women were just not factored in. And so, workplace rules and culture were largely developed to be comfortable for men, not for men and women.

A few examples of how workplaces developed as a result: Specific office hours were set even in environments where they weren't necessary to serve customers or run a factory. Since women then (and now) take on more household and family tasks, this rigid schedule made it harder for women to work. Client development activities and networking, social activities to get to know teammates and company leaders, revolved around activities like golf or socializing in a bar after work during a time when most women did not golf and did not feel comfortable or have the time to go out drinking after work. Sports and military analogies were regularly used at work to describe strategies or tactics analogies; they did not resonate with women in the same way. While we are well beyond the bygone era when most women did not work, these types of norms persist, especially in companies, including in the technology sector that still has a predominantly male workforce. Ping pong tables, video games, and beer pong are familiar in work spaces. Posters that would be more appropriate in a boy's locker room or bedroom are hung on office walls. At a recent angel investor conference, attendees were invited by a participant to a "cigars and drinks" get-together. The result from situations like these is that women are not as comfortable or as satisfied in these types of settings, and their needs are not being met.

People create culture. And people like you can change culture. You can create a better work environment for yourself and for the women you work with and care about. You don't have to wait for your company or anyone or anything to start. You are an essential missing key that can unlock the underleveraged talent pool of women. You and millions of men and women like you can change the workplace to one where both men and women have the opportunity to thrive every day working side by side.

I'd like to show you how.

Keep in Mind

One of the most important points to keep in mind while you are reading this book is that there are *many* more similarities than differences between men and women. According to Louann Brizendine, MD, American scientist, neuropsychiatrist, and author of *The Female Brain* and *The Male Brain*, "More than 99 percent of male and female genetic coding is exactly the same. But that percentage difference influences every single cell in our bodies – from the nerves that register pleasure and pain, to the neurons that transmit perception, thoughts, feelings, and emotions."[10]

The second point is that knowing that you are unconsciously biased about women does not do much. Making people aware that they are unconsciously biased has been a key strategy that many companies have unsuccessfully used to address gender imbalanced workplaces. But awareness alone does very little. Every person on the planet, men and women, including me, is unconsciously biased. The morning I started writing this introduction, I was so disappointed in myself after I realized that I had unwittingly made one of these unconscious assumptions – about a woman, no less! I was reading a *New York Times* article about a Russian attorney who met with one of President Trump's sons and some aides in the weeks leading up to the November 2016 election. As I read along, I clearly pictured a male attorney. But when I got further down the column and the attorney's name was revealed, I was shocked. The attorney was a woman. How could I, of all people, have made such a biased assumption?

To change our perception of a group of people or circumstances requires action. Clearly, I need to take more actions myself!

Unconscious bias is not an indictment. It's like an operating system that unbeknownst to you runs on autopilot in the back of your brain. Our brain can only process so much information, so it creates shortcuts using prior knowledge and experiences to make assumptions and influence our decision making. These cognitive shortcuts become our biases. Learning that we are unconsciously biased in many everyday interactions is just information.

There is evidence that educating people about their biases does very little, if anything, to reduce these biases. The way we can minimize them is by taking individual and collective action.[11] Our biases are not hardwired. And although it's not easy, we interrupt them when we act differently. While we all have biases, and *both men and women* have some negative biases toward women, the most important thing to know is that people everywhere are working hard to overcome their unconscious biases and succeeding in doing so. You can too!

People everywhere are working hard to overcome their biases through intentional action and **are succeeding** in doing so. You can too.

This book describes the individual actions that the most successful managers and leaders take to build diverse high-performing teams and equitable work environments. In this case, these actions are specifically related to one type of diversity, gender. This is not tokenism. To me gender parity does not mean only advancing women, it means men and women working equally together. Part of being a great leader and manager is treating everyone on your team fairly and equitably and creating an environment in which each person can excel.

The actions contained in this book are individual in nature. You can take them no matter what type of environment you work in and no matter what your organization or the people around you are doing or not doing. This is not a program or initiative. Your actions are not dependent on anything or anyone else. Both men and women can take these actions. But, I wrote this book primarily for men because today most managers and leaders are men and because men keep asking me what they can do to work more effectively with women.

The actions contained in this book are about working more effectively with women, but if you take them, not only will you be a better manager of women, you'll be a better manager of all types of people, including men, introverts, people of different cultures, millennials, and the incoming Generation Z.

I recognize that what I am asking you to do won't always be easy and may at times feel uncomfortable. These behaviors may be different from the familiar ways on which you and many male leaders have typically relied. They require you to step out of your comfort zone and take some risk. The women you work with and your company's leaders want you to do these things because they are important to them and good for business. As importantly, these actions also will help you be more successful in your own career and be a better colleague, manager, and leader.

If you start with a goal to be fair and operate with the beliefs that women want to advance, that having more women in the workforce will expand, not shrink, the pie of opportunity for everyone, and that when women succeed, men don't lose, you will drive better results and working conditions for yourself, as well as for the women you work with and care about. It bears repeating: When you elevate women, you also will secure your own success.

Ready?

How to Use This Book

I recommend that you:

1. Read this book once all the way through. At the end of every chapter, ask yourself: Do I take appropriate steps to intentionally advance everyone on my team? How do I recruit, retain, and advance men on my team? How does that compare to what I do to recruit, retain, and advance women on my team? What should I do differently if I want to reap the benefits of a gender-balanced team? You will find a quick self-assessment tool at the end of each of the core chapters to guide you.

2. Skim through the book again and:

   - Jot down some actions you can commit to take.

   - Pull out some ideas to share with your colleagues and teammates.

   - See if there are any sections you'd like to discuss with the women with whom you work to gain their perspective. Listen intently to what they say.

3. Keep the book on hand. When you are going into a meeting or an interview, or you are about to have a discussion with a woman, use the book and remind yourself of what she might want and

how you can be a great situational manager to her. The WE 4.0 At a Glance section and the WE 4.0 Checklist at the end of the book are designed to be quick reference guides for you.

4. If you have ideas or come up with additional actions that would be helpful to men and women in the workplace, send a note to raniaanderson@thewaywomenwork.com or tweet me @thewaywomenwork. I look forward to hearing from you.

I did not write this book to enlighten or inspire you. I wrote it to enlist you and equip you to act. If you want to understand and genuinely support gender inclusion and want fair play, if you want both the women and men you know and love to have equal opportunities and work in inclusive environments, and if you want to change the future for your son, daughter, loved ones, and colleagues, then this book is for you. As importantly, if men and women want to succeed together and prosper in this new era of work, we will need to work more effectively together. Choose whatever drives and motivates you. This book is not about what not to do. It's about what you can do. This book is not about reading; it's about action.

A gender-diverse team is a competitive advantage. It may seem counterintuitive, but when you accelerate the success of women, you accelerate your own success. If you are able to build a high-performing diverse team, your results will outpace your competition.

01

Why Care About Gender Balance at Work?

We don't care about diversity because it's in vogue. We care about it because we like winning.[1]

–*Mike Gamson,*
SVP Global Solutions, LinkedIn

You Can't Win Without Women

The way I see it, you have three choices. Each comes with an associated risk. The question is, which risks are you willing to take?

YOU can continue to operate in a work environment that is not fully inclusive of the talents and needs of women. Some men think this means less competition for them and more opportunity. The risk with this course of action is, at minimum, twofold. On one hand, women drive 70–85% of all consumer purchasing decisions through a combination of their buying power and influence. They have control of more than $20 trillion in global spending. In the United States alone, the purchasing power of women ranges from $5 trillion to $15 trillion annually. Women purchase more than 50% of goods that were formerly considered "male" products, including automobiles, home improvement tools, and consumer electronics. Women make 70% of all travel decisions. Women make 90% of household healthcare decisions. And, here's one that totally surprised me, female gamers who are age 55 and older, spend more time online gaming than males ages 15–24![2]

Without women on your team and in leadership and decision-making positions, you will have less understanding of your clients' needs. With this first approach, you risk not having the talent that your business needs. There's fierce competition for the best people. Your competitors who are doing a better job of recruiting, retaining, and advancing women will have an edge.

YOU could choose not to advance the careers of anyone on your team, male or female. Instead, you could look out for yourself exclusively. Through the years, I've known some managers and leaders whose behavior falls into this category, and you've likely also encountered them. They hire weak players, don't develop or delegate to them, hog the spotlight for themselves, and steal their people's ideas. It never works out. In the end, they shoot themselves in the foot, don't succeed, and are sometimes even fired.

YOU could build a high-performing team, which by definition is a diverse team. Under this scenario, you understand that when you work with or lead a high-performing team and team members have opportunities and do their best work, the team wins, each individual member wins, and you win.

The first two approaches are fear-based strategies. The last is based on confidence in your abilities and the abilities of others to collectively lead, manage, and excel. It's your choice which strategy you adopt.

But don't misunderstand me. The success of women does not rest only on your shoulders.

What I Tell Women

I assure you that, for all the actions that I recommend you take in this short book, I have a much longer list of career, business, and workplace actions that women can use to work more effectively with men. *Undeterred: The Six Success Habits of Women in Emerging Economies*, my career-advice book for women, is four times longer than this one. This is one indication that I'm not picking on men or suggesting that the burden for achieving a new type of workplace is entirely on their shoulders.

Men and women are engaged in a mutual transformation. I advise women to work well with men and to encourage and support men who are taking positive steps to advance women: to invite them to participate in women's initiatives, to give them a chance when they try new approaches, to give them some leeway if what they say or do is imperfect, to catch and acknowledge men when they do the right things, and not be too quick to criticize them for minor infractions of company or social rules.

I don't think it's your sole responsibility to create a work environment that is conducive to women's success. It also takes executive leadership commitment, organizational structure, practices, and benefits, and women themselves understanding, advocating, and producing results in order for all of us to achieve optimal work environments. But I also know that you are the missing and integral key to transforming the current work environment as we know it.

Addressing Possible Objections

Discussions about the advancement of women often stir up people's feelings. Objections to the approaches I advocate may come up when you're reading, so I'd like to proactively address a few you might have.

"I don't want to stereotype women." I imagine I'll be criticized by some men and women for "stereotyping" women and their needs. That is certainly not my intent, nor do I wish to oversimplify female behavior or needs. I am aware of how every woman (in fact, every person) is different based on his or her life experiences, age, national origin, personality, where he or she grew up, where he or she lives, career stage, and occupation...the list goes on and on.

My goal is to convey, as accurately as possible, some of the most common workplace needs that I've heard women express throughout my 33-year career in business, what women on every continent have personally told me, and what I've read in innumerable research papers and studies.

My approach is to present what women want, not what women are or are not. Like every man, every woman is different and has a unique personality, set of strengths, ways of interacting, motivations, goals, and so on.

"Why should I have to treat women differently?" Some readers will question why this book is even needed. Their objections may be worded something like this: "Why do women need special treatment? Why should I have to treat them differently?"

During the more than two decades that I've coached and developed managers and leaders, what's been true 100% of the time is that every management situation and every individual is different and should therefore be treated differently. The best form of management is situational in nature, an approach wherein the skills and interests of an employee are evaluated within the context of the situation, task, and goal at hand.

So, to this objection, I say: Every manager, male or female, should seek to understand as much as he or she can about the motivations, needs, and preferred communication styles of all his/her employees. My goal is to give you insights into the best-practice approaches preferred by women. You will likely encounter several women who are exceptions to these guidelines, but as a manager of women, you'll want to know how to best utilize the valuable, untapped talent pool of women.

I think about it like this: Coaches of teams want to win. As the coach of your team, I assume you want to win. Coaches of winning teams, first and foremost, get to know their players as individuals and athletes. They also rely on research about players' motivations, which may include understanding differences between how girls/women and boys/men learn and are motivated. Here's what two coaches have to say.

Julia West, PhD, a professor whose thesis dealt with intrinsic and extrinsic motivation in sports and who coaches both boys' and girls' teams, shared this insight: Boys tend to want to start playing by doing just that, starting. By contrast, girls are typically more concerned with whether they have the skills and abilities to play and want to develop those skills before they start.[3] Wade Gilbert, PhD, whose areas of expertise include athletic motivation, says: "Male athletes may be more motivated to practice and learn new skills when their performances are compared to teammates. Conversely, female athletes may respond best when their progress is charted against their own performance standards."[4]

I spoke with Dennis Casey, a senior leader at a technology company in Milwaukee, Wisconsin, who on the side, has coached 14–18-year-old girls in basketball and volleyball on a competitive level for 20 years. I asked him if he uses any coaching techniques for girls that he wouldn't likely use with boys. He immediately relayed that because the girls who he coaches attend different schools, they don't get a chance to connect during the day. So he and his assistant coaches allocate 10–15 minutes at the start of every practice for them to talk to each other in the group. He explained why. "If I did that with a group of 14-year-old boys, I'd get a bunch of perplexed faces and grunts. But for the girls, that 10 to 15 minutes helps them to feel more connected to their teammates, which is critical to *winning* a volleyball game." The point is, giving the girls those 15 minutes helps them win. When I relayed this story to a male attorney who coached boys' hockey teams for many years, he said, "Of course, it is called 'knowing what buttons to push so you can win.'"

"Some women don't want or need to be treated differently." I've heard men say that they know women who (1) tell them that they don't want to be treated differently from men, and (2) use foul language, tell raunchy jokes, and don't seem to mind when others do. Just because a woman curses or tells jokes doesn't mean she is okay with jokes that put down women or other groups of people. It is simply not appropriate to objectify women or make sexist comments. It may seem that a woman doesn't mind locker-room banter, but it may be that she is not objecting because she desperately wants to fit in or is ambitious and afraid to say anything that will hurt her prospects. The only way to know for sure that she does not object is to pointedly ask her. With regard to your perception that she does not want to treated differently, that may be the case, but everyone wants to be valued and treated with respect.

"I already treat everyone fairly." We prefer to believe that everyone has the same opportunities. We don't like to admit that we are biased or that we treat anyone unfairly.

Likely, you are already supportive of equality for men and women. But sometimes our self-perceptions are inflated. We don't recognize or understand the experiences of people who are not like us. What we think is a meritocracy is, in fact, not. And even with the best intentions, sometimes we don't say or do the right things. Most of us have not been taught how to work collaboratively and on equal footing with the opposite gender. If you objectively look at the numbers of women in key decision-making roles, you cannot help but conclude that although we might wish to believe that it is a level playing field, the data proves that it is not.

At a conference, a male investor shared with me how he has always thought of himself as fair, unbiased, and willing to invest in a business regardless of the gender, race, and age of the entrepreneur. As long as the entrepreneur had a strong business case and model, he'd consider them without reservation. But, after hearing me talk about how both men and women evaluate and describe female entrepreneurs differently from the way we describe male-led ventures, and reflecting back on the investments he'd made to date, he recognized that perhaps his approach was not as open and unbiased as he'd believed. The reality is that we all can improve. Be on the look out for the details of the study I shared in Chapter 3.

The Business Case (In Case You Don't Already Know It)

When companies hire me to speak on how they can better recruit, retain, advance, and manage women, I am always asked to make the business case for why the workplace needs more women and more women leaders, and I do make this case.

Fundamentally, men need to understand that **progression for women is not a problem for women, it's an opportunity for business.**[5]

–Andy Woodfield, PwC partner

But truth be told, I resent the request. There are no requests to prove the business case for why men should be hired and promoted – although, with the advent of artificial intelligence and spread of robotics, maybe someday there will be. And further, the business case I am making is not about "more women." It's about men and women working equally and in concert with each other.

The most provocative view I've read challenging the need to continue to have to make the business case for women comes from Adam Quinton, the founder and CEO of Lucas Ventures and an Adjunct Professor at Columbia University. He wrote:

"In my view, the 'business case' argument is an answer to the WRONG question. Rather, we should be trying to challenge the start point – namely, the assumption that men "deserve to be there." Rather than asking what the rationale is to let outsiders in, the business case question(s) should be:

- What is the business case for corporate leadership dominated by mediocre white men?

- Why does that produce better results?

- Why is that meritocratic?"[6]

No matter how we torture the data we get the same result: **women in the C-suite are associated with higher profitability.**[7]

–Marcus Noland, Director of Studies at the Peterson Institute

Today, just as we have a great deal of data about the productivity of men, we also have a significant body of evidence about the economic value of women in the workforce and in leadership positions. I could fill pages and pages with studies, research findings, and statistics that demonstrate the contributions of the full engagement and leadership of women (and indeed, I've based this book on a great deal of that research), but I'll spare you the deep dive into the weeds and share only a few highlights.

Here's the bottom line:

Just as we calculate a return on equity in business, we can also calculate a return on equality.

Diversity = Dollars.[8]

*−Christopher Mims, technology columnist
for The Wall Street Journal*

The Data in Dollars and Sense

The $12 Trillion Business Opportunity. According to McKinsey & Company, a "best in region" gender equality scenario – if all countries match the rate of improvement of the fastest-improving country in their region, in terms of gender equality – as much as *$12 trillion*, or 11%, in global annual gross domestic product (GDP) by 2025 could be added. In a "full potential" scenario, in which women play an identical role in labor markets to that of men, as much as *$28 trillion*, or 26%, could be added to global annual GDP by 2025.[9]

More equality leads to higher GDP. If we had female labor-force participation rates that were equal to male participation rates, we would have a positive net impact on GDP in both developing and developed countries. For example, India's GDP would rise an estimated 27%.

Higher gender equality rates in the workforce results in more productivity. More women working will directly increase overall productivity and indirectly lead to more investment in women's priorities, such as children's health, education, and welfare.

Gender-balanced leadership leads to better all-around performance. Companies with more women executives have greater focus on corporate governance, corporate responsibility, and talent.[10]

Companies with more women leaders have higher net revenue margins and a higher return on equity. For profitable companies, a move from 0% to 3% female leaders is associated with a 15% increase in net revenue margin. Companies with 50% women in senior operating roles show a 19% higher rate of return on equity on average.[11]

Improved gender balance on boards of directors results in better share prices and financial performance. This finding was further confirmed in the International Finance Corporation's April 2017 Investing in Women Study, which concluded that companies with diverse boards generate a higher return on equity and in terms of share price, and that higher performing companies are 50% more likely to give both men and women equal influence on strategy.[12]

The benefits of diversity are not one-sided. They don't flow only to the group of people being included (in this case, women). For example, some of the ways that gender parity benefits men are: removing the burden for men to be the sole economic providers for their families; providing opportunities for men to pursue all types of jobs, not just jobs that were traditionally considered appropriate for men; raising family income levels; allowing men to more fully engage with their families and children; and creating equal opportunity for their daughters, spouses, mothers, and sisters. A more diverse workforce benefits *you*.

We don't need more studies and data to support why we need more women in leadership roles and in the workforce. What we need is more action to achieve an egalitarian workplace and gender-balanced leadership. What we need is a novel new approach that includes your proactive, personal engagement.

An engineering company executive recently attended a meeting at the offices of a key client. He brought an all-male team to the meeting. The engineering firm specializes in infrastructure development in power, oil and gas, water, and telecommunications, and has projects around the world. Being awarded projects of the magnitude delivered by this firm requires a very long sales cycle and a tremendous amount of expertise and experience. Connecting and building relationships with potential clients during this long sales and project-delivery period is imperative to their success. The executive has a proven history of developing these types of relationships. But this time he noticed something different.

When he and his team walked into the meeting, the client team seated around the table was diverse in terms of age, gender, and race. He realized then and there that his company was not going to be able to use the same tactics nor rely solely on the same people it had in the past to develop the type of rapport and relationship needed to be awarded proposals in the future. That's the bottom line and the business case.

02

The WE 4.0 Framework

I think about global efforts to achieve gender equality as having gone through three stages of providing rights for women:

1.0 Political and property rights

2.0 Social rights

3.0 Workplace rights

These hard-won rights were the required stepping stones to get women where we are today. Notwithstanding notable and glaring exceptions in some countries, women, overall, have made significant strides in education, health, voting and property rights, equal pay, the workplace, and more.

But now, the march to gender equality is stalled, especially in terms of economic participation.

WOMEN aren't advancing any further and, in fact, in the 10 years since the World Economic Forum began measuring it, the global economic gender gap has narrowed by only 2%.[1]

CONTRARY to widely held beliefs, global rates of female labor-force participation have stagnated, or even fallen, in recent decades.[2]

ALTHOUGH millennials are confident they will be the generation to achieve gender parity,[3] the World Economic Forum reports that in 2017 the global gender gap actually widened, and that it will take a staggering 217 more years to close it.[4]

Klaus Schwab, founder and chairman of the World Economic Forum, sees that the world is on the brink of a fourth industrial revolution. He describes this period as a "Technological revolution that will fundamentally alter the way we live, work, and relate to one another. We do not yet know just how it will unfold, but one thing is clear: the response to it must be integrated and comprehensive, involving all stakeholders of the global polity, from the public and private sectors to academia and civil society."[5]

This integrated approach to development in the fourth industrial revolution will also require men and women to relate differently to each other. From my perspective, successfully operating in the fourth industrial revolution necessitates that we also achieve the fourth and final stage of the gender movement: gender equality. Fully utilizing the talents and leadership of women is part of the next frontier of global economic prosperity.

WE 4.0 is for all of us: women and men, working equally, sharing leadership and succeeding together. No longer can women carry the flag or bear the sole responsibility for leading the charge to gender equality. What businesses need now is men and women leading equally and working side by side to drive innovation, opportunity, and prosperity. WE 4.0 is your hands-on guide to improve the way men and women lead and succeed together.

Women and men must be equal partners in managing the challenges our world faces – and in reaping the opportunities. Both voices are critical in ensuring the Fourth Industrial Revolution delivers its promise for society.[6]

–Klaus Schwab, Founder and Executive Chairman of the World Economic Forum

How good would it feel to be able to leverage an underutilized strategy to drive your own results and career? How good would you feel to know that both men and women were being treated equally in your workplace? How good would it feel not to be blamed for the inequitable treatment of women? How good would it feel to know that your wife or girlfriend or daughter had the same opportunities as her male colleagues? How wonderful would it be if your business took off because you had a more diverse team that was better at solving problems, understanding customers, and identifying opportunities? How good would it feel to know that you personally contributed to the achievement of gender parity globally? These are the types of outcomes I had in mind when I wrote this book to guide a new way for men and women to work together.

Like many, my vision is of true egalitarianism at work. A day when people in every workplace have the opportunity to leverage their strengths, achieve their full potential, and share leadership.

WE 4.0

EXPAND

ELIMINATE

ENCOURAGE

ENGAGE

The WE 4.0 Framework

The origins of the WE 4.0 framework are inspired by and built on my more than two decades of experience coaching and developing businessmen and businesswomen, observing what works and what does not; on listening deeply to what women all over the world regularly tell me they want or don't want from their managers and colleagues at work; and on the research and findings of many other leading experts and institutions, especially Dr. Elisabeth Kelan, PhD, a Professor of Leadership at Cranfield School of Management and Director of the Cranfield International

Centre for Women Leaders[7]; McKinsey & Company; Avivah Wittenberg-Cox, the CEO of 20-first, a leading gender consultancy, and an authority on leadership, gender, and business; and Catalyst, the global nonprofit renowned for its research and thought leadership in building inclusive workplaces that work for women. My goal was to distill research and experience into actions that you can take as you go about normal work.

The framework contains four categories of intentional individual behavior to enable you to maximize your own success and business results by proactively working more effectively with women and by recruiting, retaining, and advancing more women into leadership.

Remember, WE 4.0 is about your behavior. You don't have to wait for your organization or anyone else to implement a program or change anything before you can take these actions. You merely have to decide to do so. But these behaviors are not one-time actions. To affect change, you'll need to make these behaviors habitual and consistently interact with women in these ways.

I recognize that transformational change is hard and that no one can make you change if you don't truly want to or see the need for it. Change is especially hard when the status quo, our current environment, appears to be working positively for us. But, while it may seem that the current environment is working for you, it's actually not. Inequality is bad for business; it's bad for everyone, and it's not sustainable. We are all missing out on so many opportunities.

Take a few minutes to think about why you might want to take the actions described in this book. Are your goals oriented around your own advancement, your company's long-term success, understanding the needs of your customers, reflecting your customer base, fairness, your community, equality, and/or your family? You'll have to figure out what motivates and drives you so you can start to:

ELIMINATE. Stop behaviors and practices that negatively impact women.

EXPAND. Interact with women in a more frequent, intentional, and impactful way.

ENCOURAGE. Support and prompt women to take advantage of high-impact opportunities and achieve their full potential.

ENGAGE. Take advantage of employee and work-life benefits available to you and participate in initiatives that elevate women. Be an ally.

Dr. Elisabeth Kelan describes an outcome of implementing these types of behaviors as *undoing gender*.[8]

How WE 4.0 Helps You

As you read along, you'll see how using WE 4.0 behaviors has helped many different types of people. Our larger motivations and rationales for wanting to have a more equal work environment for everyone are complex, interrelated, and will require commitment from all of us. On a simpler, more individual level, if one of your motivations is achieving results and getting ahead in your career or business, you'll need to think strategically. In fact, the ability to think strategically is a prerequisite skill for either entrepreneurial success or advancement in a corporate setting. Figure 2.1 shows levels of decision making in the organization.

One of the most important actions of successful executives or entrepreneurs in building a high-growth company is the ability to make strategic decisions. A manager who doesn't think strategically about ways to recruit, retain, and advance talent won't be able to make the best business decisions, let alone secure his own success. WE 4.0 actions are designed to help you think strategically about the talents of women, about building a diverse, high-performing team, and to set yourself up for career and business growth.

Figure 2.1: **Decision Pyramid**

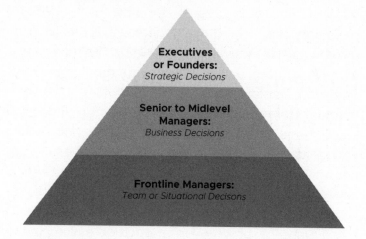

Executives or Founders:
Strategic Decisions

Senior to Midlevel Managers:
Business Decisions

Frontline Managers:
Team or Situational Decisons

It's time to think and act differently. As you know, adopting new behaviors is not easy. Consistently using them – making them habits – is even harder. When I want to adopt new behaviors, I start by figuring out what I should first stop doing to make room for what I want to start doing. So, let's begin to *ELIMINATE*.

What's the business case for keeping the status quo? Inequality is bad for business, and it's bad for everyone.

03

Eliminate

Eliminate behaviors and practices that disproportionately and negatively impact women.

ELIMINATE

What Women Want

- A level playing field

- To be valued and respected

- No discrimination or sexual harassment

- To be judged on their performance (output and results), not on their presence (hours) in the office

The Problem

Some workplace practices and behaviors disproportionately impact women.

Some customary practices, like regularly scheduling 7:00 a.m. meetings, are seemingly benign. But such practices usually adversely impact women more than men because they are more likely the ones seeing their kids off to school or day care.

Others are even more harmful. While instances of overt discrimination or harassment of women may have declined in past decades, the recent outpouring of women sharing awful experiences painfully reminds us that it's still occurring. Today, bias against women is primarily unconscious or manifests in the form of microaggressions that are not fully recognized or understood.

Macroaggression occurs on a systemic level, for instance, in the form of unequal pay practices or conditions for a certain group of people. In contrast, microaggressions are intentional or unintentional verbal or nonverbal behaviors that occur in everyday interactions, which are often unacknowledged and casually degrade, demean, or put down someone who is part of a group (for instance, a gender, race, or ethnic group).[1]

According to a 2015 report on gender bias in the G20 nations from British international policy institute Chatham House, "Gender bias perpetuates low expectations of women's human value and capabilities."[2]

Gender microaggressions include sexual objectification, the use of sexist language, making assumptions based on gender, the use of sexist humor, slights, insults, or using a derogatory analogy. Here's a blatant example that I can't forget: Clémentine Pirlot, a software developer in Paris, posted a message online about a time when she and her male colleagues gathered to have a drink together after work. Later that evening, when the director of the team joined them, he said: "Move over, I need room for my big d—k."[3] (His word rhymes with kick and refers to the male sexual organ.)

The blatant, more obvious incidents like Clémentine's are easy to spot. But what about the much more prevalent kind, the ones that are much harder to notice unless you are like IT and Innovation Manager Sasha Shlieienkov, and you are more aware and start looking?

I gave a keynote presentation to group of 40 male and 40 women business leaders about how they could better recruit, retain, and advance women and work more effectively together. We had the same number of men and women because we made it a registration requirement that in order to attend, you had to sign with a colleague of the opposite sex. Before the session started, a man in his early 30s came up to greet me and told me how eager he was to hear my presentation, and how he had cleared his schedule in order to be able to attend. After the session, he came back up to thank me for sharing such helpful tips. He's trying to be a good guy by learning about how to work more effectively with women and by supporting women entrepreneurs.

Then he spotted a male entrepreneur he knew. The entrepreneur was talking to a young female IT professional. They were deep in conversation on an important topic, but to the businessman who had just spoken to me, the young woman was invisible. He jumped right in and began talking to the male entrepreneur. He did not acknowledge, recognize, or greet the young woman. He did not apologize for interrupting her.

When he left, the entrepreneur, the woman and her manager, Sasha Shlieienkov, were quiet and reflective. We didn't know why the man failed to acknowledge the woman – gender, age, excitement about seeing his friend, or just plain oversight? Sasha told me that before my session he would not have noticed the incident, and that likely over the years there were hundreds of similar interactions. He wished he had said something. The woman wished she had said something. I often wish I could say just the right thing. It's hard. It takes preparation and practice and, even with both, it still takes courage.

Here are six common types of microaggressions toward women:

1. **Calling women by seemingly endearing names that are not appreciated and which some women even find offensive**. For example, the leader of a very large company in Latin America shared with me how much she hates it when one colleague calls her *reina* (queen).

2. **Describing women's actions in ways that would not be used to describe men who did the same things**. For example: labeling a woman as too nice to be able to do a job, bossy, a drama queen, too aggressive, needy, high-strung, and so on. As one woman at a New York City tech start-up company told me, "I'm constantly aware that I am the only women who works at the company, as I am regularly told how much 'nicer' I am to work with than any of the other guys at my company." Although this may seem like a compliment, that's not how most women would take it. Women who negotiate for a promotion or an increase in their compensation are 30% more likely to receive feedback that they are "bossy," "too aggressive," or

"intimidating" than men who negotiated for the terms of their compensation.[4]

Observations of venture capitalists (VCs) in Sweden, of all places – one of the most gender-equal countries in the world – show just how differently men and women are sometimes viewed. Entrepreneurs who pitched during 2009 and 2010 were described in the following ways: Male entrepreneurs were described as "young and promising" whereas women were thought of as "young and inexperienced"; men were described as "experienced and knowledgeable," but women as "experienced but worried"; men were described as "cautious, sensible, and level-headed," while women were "too cautious and unsure."[5]

3. **Believing and acting as if women are weak and need the protection of men**. One example of this is thinking or saying that a woman would not want the same type of stress, workload, or challenging assignment as a man. Psychologists Peter Glick, PhD, and Susan Fiske, PhD, call this *benevolent sexism*. Their research indicates that men who exhibit this type of microaggression are less likely to give women candid feedback and challenging assignments, two management actions that are critical to women's advancement and that you'll read more about in the next chapter.[6]

4. **Characterizing a woman as too emotional or unstable, especially if you are being challenged or questioned by her**. For example, calling a woman a nag, telling her to calm down, or saying things like: "I don't know why you are so upset" or "You are such a diva."

5. **Touching women without their consent**. You would think that this could go without saying, but it still happens. Unless it's completely acceptable in your culture, you should not touch people you work with. An example of when it is acceptable is in countries where people automatically kiss each other's cheeks when they meet. In that case, you'd want to greet women according to culturally accepted norms. The only question in these circumstances could be, is it one, two, or three kisses? In all other circumstances, even though your intentions may be completely harmless and even supportive, physical contact, like putting you hand on a woman's shoulder, should be avoided.

As for putting your hand on a woman's butt – well, that should never happen! Believe me, I witnessed just that at a work gathering, and it was caught on camera! In case you are wondering what happened, yes, the man who did it was fired. It was the third inappropriate incident, and he already had been reprimanded, instructed, and given two earlier chances to improve his conduct.

6. **Making sexually laden innuendos about or to women**. Here are a few examples of conversations relayed to me.

- Between two men in an open office environment: Male A: "That was a short call with X (female) client." Male B: "Yeah, seven minutes plus cuddling."

- During a lunch meeting, a man admonished his female coworker by saying, "You can't even order because you're all nervous staring at the good-looking waiter."

- A freelancer who worked with us would come in and without fail ask my female coworker if she was "getting any." He asked her that same question every time he saw her.

Some of these subtle and not-so-subtle actions or comments may not seem like a big deal and one incident in isolation may not be. In reality, these types of incidents inhibit women from doing their best work and undermine their success. Women cite these types of disrespectful, sometimes toxic behaviors as one of the factors that influence their decisions to leave a job. A steady diet of microaggression disconnects and wears women down. When they cite these types of behaviors as factoring into a reluctant decision to leave a job they otherwise like, they describe it as "death by a thousand cuts."

Unintended Consequences

When a coaching client of mine became the head of technology and information at the company where she worked, she joined an all-male executive team. The team enjoyed surfing together and invited her to join them. That was great. They had included her in their camaraderie building. But when she arrived at the beach, she found out that there was no place for her to change. Although at first she felt uncomfortable, she quickly came up with a novel solution. She asked the men to get in a circle with their arms outstretched to hold their towels up with their backs turned toward her. She then got in the middle of the circle and changed. My client was a great sport about it, yet the truth is that she still felt uncomfortable.

These are the types of awkward situations in which women find themselves that over time can disconnect them from their workplace colleagues.

The guys did the right thing by including their female colleague in their teambuilding activity. They just needed to take one more step and think about the environment from her perspective.

Future Planning: Take a few minutes to think through an activity, event, or meeting in advance with the women on your team or your wife/sister/girlfriend. Think through whether your planned activity will feel welcoming to everyone. Better yet, come up with an event or activity by asking a diverse group of people for their ideas. If all else fails, at least bring a pop-up tent or equivalent.

SOLUTIONS – WHAT WORKS

At a Glance
Actions You Can Take

Eliminate:

- Discrimination, bias, and microaggressions toward women

- Sexual harassment; in fact, eliminate any type of harassment

- Workplace practices that disproportionately and adversely impact women

- Any gender-related wage gap

What One Leader Did

Waiting to enter an important meeting with her boss, a woman heard a man say, "It's a good thing someone brought a woman along, in case we need coffee." While her boss also overheard the remark, he didn't say anything. The woman was so upset by the comment maker and even more so by her boss, that she didn't say a single word during the entire meeting.

At the end of the meeting, the man who made the comment asked the woman's boss if they could count on his business. The boss responded, "Absolutely not! The decision maker here is my colleague (*pointing to the woman*), and you completely blew your chances to do business with us prior to the meeting." With that, he stood up, motioned to his female colleague and walked out, leaving a significant business opportunity on the table.

Outside the meeting, the boss told his female colleague, "Had I said something to him about his remark when he made it, it might have embarrassed him, but he'd likely do it again. I had to do something that he and everyone else would not forget. I had to hit him where he'd really feel it – in his business results and pocket."

What You Can Do

Move from focusing on exclusively on tasks TO focusing on results and relationships. Start by evaluating and improving your own behavior before you focus on the conduct of others.

How?

Evaluate and adjust common workplace practices. Assess your team and office norms and adapt them so they don't negatively impact any group of employees.

> *Step 1*. List your team practices and norms. For instance, meeting times, networking interactions, teambuilding activities, customer events.

> *Step 2*. Ask your team members if any of the items on the list are negatively impacting them. (This will help all team members, not just women.)

> *Step 3*. Make adjustments, if at all possible.

Here are some examples of adjustments you could make:

- Out of recognition of the lifestyle of the parents in his workplace, one executive prohibits anyone in his division from scheduling regular meetings that start any time after 4:00 p.m. Of course, if there's an important reason, like an urgent customer need, for why a meeting needs to start after 4:00 p.m., then that's when the meeting will be held. This may seem like a small or inconsequential action, but even seemingly insignificant actions you take to create an environment where all your teammates can excel will have a ripple effect.

- Hold networking, customer, or teambuilding events in places where everyone, including women, feel comfortable. Don't use exclusively male social gatherings to discuss business. And definitely don't ditch a female coworker after a business dinner to go to a strip club with your male colleagues, as recently happened to a woman I know.

- If there's only one member of the opposite sex being included, don't have team/strategy/business planning sessions where everyone stays overnight in a house. In case you are surprised by this example, I assure you it is true. Several women I've spoken with have told me how often it has happened to them and how uncomfortable they've been.

Start with any action you feel comfortable taking. It will help you take other steps that improve your gender intelligence, work environment, leadership, and results.

Conduct an annual compensation review of your team members. Sort by gender (and other criteria that would help you identify any inadvertent discrepancies. You don't have to wait for your company or HR to do a salary review, you can do one for your team. Compare by position, experience, performance. If you find a misalignment, work with your leadership team to address it.

While we like to think that there are no longer differences in what men and women are paid for the same job, we've seen through the example of proactive companies that include Salesforce that unfortunately they do persist. Benioff, the CEO of Salesforce, has regularly required these types of reviews and has made millions of dollars in adjustments to ensure gender pay equity.

When women make the same amount of money as men for the same work, in addition to the increase in fairness, there is the increase in income that translates to more money flowing into the economy and spent on goods and services, increasing business and growth for others.

Recognize your own behavior and interrupt your unconscious biases. Gender bias is one of our most ingrained biases. We begin to develop our feelings and opinions about men and women, boys and girls from an early age. Our perspectives are formed by a host of experiences, including how we were brought up, what our parents told us or didn't tell us, what our parents did (and do), who our friends were (and are), and who our parents' friends were (and are) and what they did (and do), as well as through messages we see in the media throughout our lives.

Moreover, we get mixed and incomplete messages about how to collaborate with, compete with, and support members of the opposite sex. At school, we both cooperate with and compete with our classmates. On sports fields, women and men play separately and rarely compete with one another. We form friendships with members of the opposite sex, but these friendships often come under various types of pressure. Then we get to the world of work and it's a whole new game, one for which we aren't well prepared. It's tough.

Since I grew up in the Middle East and India and spent many years researching and working in emerging economies, I am also acutely aware of the additional onerous influences that patriarchal societies have on conscious and unconscious gender bias.

Here are a few actions you can take to reduce two of the most common types of unconscious gender bias.

Notice how you describe women. If you find yourself thinking or describing a woman in a work setting as too ambitious, bossy, emotional, timid, needy, or pretty, do as follows.

Step 1. Ask yourself, "Would I say that about a man in the same circumstance?"

Kristen Pressner, the global head of Human Resources for the Diagnostic Division of Roche calls this the "Flip It to Test It" approach.[7] For example, when talking with a woman about her business plans, ask yourself if these are the same questions you'd ask a man. And, when posing questions to women, don't focus on what can go wrong if you typically ask men about the upside of their plans. Remember the study about the questions that VCs ask that is discussed in the Introduction.

Step 2. Describe the impact of her behavior without labeling it.

Example: "It's difficult for me to give my full attention to what you are saying when you raise your voice."

Don't assume that a woman who only works in the office during "regular" business hours works less than or is less ambitious than her coworkers who spend more time in the office. The value assigned to the number of hours worked in the office is a hot button for some managers, particularly baby boomer managers and executives.

Focusing unduly on the number of hours an employee works in the office is an outdated practice. The paradigm has shifted. The important questions in today's environment is whether your employees interact effectively with one another. Do they coordinate and collaborate? Do they anticipate and address customer needs? Do they produce the desired level of results? A woman (or, for that matter, anyone) who doesn't spend extra time in the office or asks for a flexible schedule may be working at home at night, early in the morning, and/or on weekends. She may be more productive in a shorter amount of time than her peers.

Your employees will appreciate it when you recognize their needs and are flexible with their schedules. Your accommodations increase their loyalty to the organization and positively impact employee retention. Often requests for flexibility don't last forever, so you don't need to put a woman who makes a case for a flexible schedule in the "mommy-track" category. (More on this topic in the next chapter.)

Think differently about who is or is not in the office. An alternative way to think about time invested by your employees is to ask these types of questions: Do people get their work done and go beyond expectations offering new ideas and value? Do they work well with their colleagues? Are they available in situations where they have to be? For example, if you are a partner at a law firm, are the associates working with you on a case available for long hours, client meetings, and when a judge requires? Are they responsive to customer needs and your requests? If the answers to these types of questions are yeses, then unless your team works in places like a retail establishment, factory, or call center, it should not matter if your employee generally arrives at the office at the start of the work day and leaves right on time.

Over the course of your career, any number of circumstances may cause you not to want to or be able to put in as many hours in the office. If you create a flexible, but accountable, work environment for women, everyone will benefit, including you.

Acknowledge and apologize for your own inappropriate remarks or behavior. It is bound to happen, it happens to all of us, including me. For example, I tend to call people by endearing names and reach out to touch them on the arm or shoulder. I know I need to be very aware of when it's okay to do so or not, but sometimes I act instinctively.

You are going to slip up, not think through something you are saying spontaneously, or incorrectly assume something you have said is funny when it's not. Everybody does. Here's an example relayed to me by an American male executive. He was on the phone with some of his senior managers discussing a payment due from a client in the Middle East. In an effort to lighten an otherwise tense moment, he said, "Well, at least they are not trying to pay us with a harem." When the words were barely out of his mouth, he realized how completely inappropriate the comment was, being both derogatory to people from the Middle East and to women. He immediately apologized to everyone. But he still felt badly and knew this was not the type of example he aspired to set for his team. I heard about a group of male friends who, after seeing the prevalence of #MeToo posts on social media, got together with their female friends to ask if any of them had said or done anything inappropriate or offensive to women in the past. If so, they wanted to apologize.

The more aware you are of the phenomenon of gender microaggression, the less likely you will be to make one. But if you do, don't pretend it did not happen or invalidate the person's feelings feelings by saying something like "don't make this into a big deal" or "you are overacting." And definitely don't tell a woman you offended something like: "I thought you wanted to be one of the guys," or "Well, if you don't like it, you can always leave."

Look at a woman's eyes, face, and body language to determine if you have offended her. If you aren't sure of her reaction, ask her, "Did I just offend you?"

Acknowledge what you said or did right away. Look directly at the person you aggrieved, and apologize directly to her. Recognize that she feels insulted. Don't just apologize about the situation, as high-profile men caught in shameful actions toward women often do. Apologize *to her*. You could say, "I am sorry..."

- "That came out wrong."

- "What came out of my mouth was not at all what I intended."

- "I realize that's not at all funny."

- "That was totally inappropriate."

- "I have offended you, and that's terrible."

Furthermore, tell your female coworkers that you want to treat every woman (and person) with respect, but if you ever inadvertently offend her, you would greatly appreciate it if she would be direct with you and bring it to your attention.

Address bias, discrimination, and microaggression that you see or hear. Some airports and public places have posted signs that say, "If you see something, say something." That's the same advice to follow if you witness bias or discrimination. You are not a bystander. You are a witness. Don't ignore a biased comment, demeaning language, or inappropriate humor used in person or sent digitally. Since companies can be held legally liable for harassment of their employees by external parties that they know about, you will need to also address actions taken by your clients, vendors, or suppliers against anyone at your company. It will not be easy, but it will be easier if you've thought about and prepared some possible responses in advance.

Your goals should be to stop the offender, if possible address their behavior, and express concern for the person who was inappropriately treated. Here are a few things you could say or do:

- At the very minimum, don't laugh.

- Give the offender a disapproving look.

- Take a cue from young people who are fond of simply saying "Not cool."

- Ask, "Are you saying ... ?" Repeat verbatim what the person said, to allow them the opportunity to hear and recognize the inappropriateness of their remark.

- Ask them to explain. Say, "What do you mean by ... ?" Insert verbatim what the person said so they will be forced to explain their comment.

- Appeal to their self-perception. Say, "I've always thought you were a fair person."

- Stop the conversation. Say, "Don't speak like that in front of me."

- Stop the meeting and say, "We don't speak/act like that here."

- Ask, "Why do you think that's funny?"

- Label the behavior. "That was ... [inappropriate; sexist; harassment]"

- Say, "Don't be a jerk."

- Ask, "Would you like someone to say this about your wife, daughter, mother?"

- Express concern for the person who was inappropriately treated.

Dr. Michael Kimmel, a Distinguished Professor of Sociology and Gender Studies at Stony Brook University, and the founder of the Center for the Study of Men and Masculinities, explains that the role of men in these types of situations is not to rescue women but to challenge other men.[8] Taking these types of actions or saying these things will be helpful to you in addressing bias or discrimination toward anyone on your team, not just those leveled against women.

I won't minimize the difficulty of taking some of these actions or saying these things, especially when you are confronting other people's microaggressions and if you know you've behaved somewhat similarly in the past. You may feel that calling out someone else's behavior is hypocritical. You may worry that you will be ridiculed or ostracized by your peers. Yet you are capable of taking a stand, even if it's tough. It's the right thing to do, and it's important. Start with one action you can take, and build from there. Every elimination of a microaggression or a macroaggression helps. Every micro affirmation makes a difference.

Five-Minute Self-Assessment

Answer the following questions. Jot down some notes. Reflect on your responses. Commit to take an action or make a change.

- What words or actions have I recently taken that have sent the right messages?

- Which of my behaviors, if any, have sent the wrong messages?

- Do I confront customers and colleagues regarding uninvited sexual advances or comments toward female coworkers?

- How does what I say about my female coworkers compare to what I say about the men

I work with? For example: Do I describe a woman as "too aggressive" or "too timid" under circumstances where I would not use the same descriptor for a man's behavior?

- Do I factor hours in the office as a primary determinant of how I assess an employee's performance, or do I base performance ratings on actual results and values?

- Do my regular office practices adversely impact women or any other group of people?

Summary

Eliminate practices or words that are barriers to women's success to create a more inclusive environment.

Be mindful and vigilant. Have your emotional antenna up. Recognize and address the slightest signs of discrimination, bias, and microaggression. Ask for feedback.

Eliminating harmful behaviors and practices is a beginning, but it will only get us so far. It's merely a "do no harm" baseline. But you can't thrive only by removing or cutting. To build a high-performing team and get the results you want, you must *EXPAND*.

04

Expand

Expand your professional and business interactions with women.

EXPAND

What Women Want

- To be equally considered for challenging, high-profile opportunities and career advancement

- To be included in formal and informal networking

- To be given direct feedback

- To have access to senior leaders

- To be sponsored in addition to being mentored

The Problem

Many managers believe that women have equal opportunities in the workplace because their companies have inclusive and family-friendly practices, like maternity leave or family leave, equal pay standards, and women's leadership development programs. But that's not the case.

Removing structural barriers to women's success is imperative, yet insufficient. To change the status quo, we must also remove social barriers and improve our day-to-day interactions.

It's easier for all of us to interact with and give feedback to people who are most like us (in terms of gender, race, age, and so on). Since most managers and leaders are men, this means that male managers interact less frequently with the women in their offices than they do with the men.

Further, an analysis of 80 different studies revealed that women were more effective leaders in female-dominated and female-oriented settings, and that men were more effective leaders in male-dominated and male-oriented settings.[1]

When men believe in men, they champion them, give them direct feedback, and offer them challenging opportunities. Women want the same advantages.

Women in the Workplace 2016 study surveying the HR practices of 132 companies and 34,000 employees, **women reported that despite asking for informal feedback as often as men do, they receive it less frequently.**[2]

Unintended Consequences

A male C-suite executive of a large, global firm, who was one of my coaching clients, went with four senior leaders (three men and one woman) to a strategy meeting with a prospective client. The team's presentation missed the mark, and the meeting did not go well. Immediately afterward, while standing at the urinals in the men's bathroom, my client gave the three men on his team some heated and direct feedback about what they had done wrong and what to do differently the next time.

At our next coaching session, my client relayed what had happened and told me that he fully intended to share his reactions with the female leader soon, but he was reluctant to call her to his office, fearing that she would feel singled out. He wanted to wait for the "right time" to talk to her. Although I encouraged him not to wait too long and during a subsequent coaching session asked him whether he'd had the conversation yet, he still had "not gotten around to it."

Not long afterward, the same team had an opportunity to pitch to a similar type of prospect. Not surprisingly, the male team members were well prepared and on point, but the woman took the same ineffective approach she'd taken the first time since she hadn't received any feedback on how to improve.

My client was well intentioned. He was sensitive about not singling out the woman on his team, but he acted out of anger and in haste. After the unsuccessful meeting, he took the first opportunity he could to give some members of his team feedback. And of course, they needed to hear it. But he should have not said anything in the bathroom and waited until everyone was together to give his feedback. And the woman's male coworkers should have shared their boss's feedback with her. The woman should have also asked for specific feedback from her boss.

If you do inadvertently vent or blow off steam in a place where only part of the team is gathered, as happens to many of us, be sure you follow up with everyone not present. It's bad management not to regularly debrief with your full team after a disaster or a home-run.

Future Planning: One effective way to give immediate actionable feedback after client or external meetings is to institute a practice commonly called *curbside coaching*. Everyone gets together right after the meeting for a quick debrief of what went well and what didn't, and to discuss what to do differently next time and outline the next steps. And, no final feedback at the urinals!

SOLUTIONS – WHAT WORKS

At a Glance
Actions You Can Take

Expand:

- How you recruit women

- The number of female candidates you consider for a job or opportunity

- How frequently you interact and network with women

- Your professional network and connections with women

- The direct feedback and challenging assignments you give women, to be comparable to what you say and provide their male counterparts

- How you sponsor and invest in high-performing, high-potential women

What One Leader Did

One day, while walking around the Dubai shop floor of Cummins, one of the world's largest engine manufacturers, Rachid Ouenniche, the managing director of Africa/Middle East distribution, observed that there were no women working in a certain area. He asked the factory manager, "Is there a reason why women could not work in this area?"

The manager thoughtfully considered the question and replied, "No, no reason."

A few months later, on another visit to the floor of the factory, the CEO saw two women working in that part of the shop.

Over a five-year period, the ratio of female employees at Cummins increased from 10% to 22%. Ouenniche focused the company's efforts on recruiting more women, including through the implementation of a university internship program in which one of the first cohorts of 18 interns included 16 women. He also made a point of being actively engaged with the young women at the beginning of their careers.

I spoke to Ouenniche when he was part of a panel of male CEOs that I facilitated at a conference in November 2015 in Abu Dhabi, and it was evident that his personal involvement made a notable difference. He framed it like this in an article in *The National*: "I talk to them (the women), and I ensure that their mentors, sponsors, and managers know how important this is. Personal engagement and involvement by senior leadership is essential, because these are our future leaders. If we take a long view, and focus on the pipeline, it tells us we will be more successful as a business."[3]

What You Can Do

Move from a passive, reactive, occasional approach to recruiting women and developing the women on your team ("the company is taking care of women" approach) TO a proactive, intentional, consistent approach, in which you could say: "I personally give women the opportunities and feedback they need to excel and lead in my/our company."

How?

In a room filled with business leaders, most of whom were dressed in business suits, a tech entrepreneur in jeans and sweater stood up and asked me for help. He explained that he has several job openings and would love to fill some with women. His goal was not to "help" women. He did not ask "Why don't the women apply?" Instead he brilliantly asked "What can I change so women will apply?" He wants to fill his openings with great talent and build a successful business. He wasn't looking for people with a specific list of technical qualifications because what his company does is so new that hardly anyone has any experience in the field. He just needed people who wanted to learn. He had paired down the qualifications listings in the job postings, but still his candidate pool was almost exclusively men. We brainstormed ideas, including many of the ones you'll read here, and even talked about taking overt measures by placing some ads that used a bit of humor and included phrases like: "Women Wanted" or "Women Please Apply" or "Technical Skills Not Required" or "All Applicants Encouraged to Apply Regardless of Technical Skills."

Consider using the following types of sourcing and recruiting strategies and tactics.

Assess your recruiting practices and proactively recruit women. A partner at McKinsey & Company shared an experience that changed his beliefs and actions related to conscious gender inclusion. After showing up at a meeting with an all-male team of experts, his client pointedly and in frustration asked whether this team was diverse enough to see all sides of the client's problem.[4]

Some managers justify their reactive approach by saying there aren't enough women or saying that women don't apply. That's one approach. The other is to use the approach the tech entrepreneur used and ask the question "what are *we* doing or not doing that results in us not having women candidates?"

As sociologist and political economist Mauro Guillén, PhD, Wharton Management Professor and Director of the Lauder Institute, wisely points out, "If you don't hire, attract, and retain women executives ... you are discarding half the talent pool graduating from business schools."[5] And if you're not hiring them, your competitors are.

Sometimes, unconscious bias against women is a form of *status quo bias,* a bias to default to what currently is and how things currently are. Inertia and the ease of doing things the way they've been done are very powerful enticements.[6] Most recruiting practices have been unconsciously built with men as the default option.

There are good reasons to resist the lure of the familiar. "One of the most pivotal things that men can do is champion feminine skills and competencies that we all possess and are now essential to succeed in a social, open, and interconnected society," asserts John Gerzema, author of *The Athena Doctrine.*[7]

Don't blame a "nonexistent" pipeline. Go beyond making symbolic or perfunctory efforts that have the appearance that you are trying to recruit more women. Your responsibility is to produce results. Ask yourself if you have overlooked or are not looking broadly enough to attract and retain the talent you need for your own success. Instead of thinking that there is a "pipeline" problem, meaning that there aren't enough women to hire, actively and genuinely commit to make your recruiting efforts more inclusive:

- Audit your job descriptions. Use gender-neutral or gender-inclusive wording in job descriptions or ads. A study of more than 4,000 job descriptions showed that words influence how men and women perceive job opportunities. Men were more drawn to words like *dominant* and *boasts,* while women preferred words like *community, relationships,* and *satisfied*. The term *hacker* was perceived as less inclusive than *developer*.[8]

See Table 4.1 for a few examples of how you can make job ads more gender inclusive.

- Ensure that your website, photos you use, recruitment materials, and the people who interview candidates are diverse and inclusive. Kat Matfield created an online job and gender decoder tool you can use to evaluate the language of your ads. It is available at http://gender-decoder.katmatfield .com.

Table 4.1 **Gender Inclusion Chart**

Less gender inclusive	More gender inclusive
Competitive environment	Competitive industry with a collaborative working environment
Address client needs	Build relationships with clients and satisfy their needs
Crush the competition	Win in the marketplace
Emphasizing long work hours	Emphasizing a focus on results in a flexible work-environment.

- Don't fill your posted job ads with a laundry list of qualifications or experiences that very few people have. Women are less likely than men to apply for jobs for which they feel they are not fully qualified, so you'll inadvertently limit highly qualified women from applying.

- Experiment with having all applications or resumes presented without a person's name or any gender identification indicators. See if that leads to different candidate selection decisions.

- Hunt for female candidates in unlikely places. Here are a few ideas. Ask your colleagues, clients, friends, and family members (especially your wife, daughter, sister, and mother) to connect you with talented women they know. Think about women you interact with in your volunteer positions, on a board of directors, in social setting, and in religious activities. Reach out to university alumni networks.

- Don't just wait for women to apply. Approach qualified women you know, and tell them you consider them a strong candidate for a role (more on this in Chapter 5). Actively search for women who may have been overlooked at your company, perhaps because they have a different background than is generally considered for the type of role you are filling, have not raised their hands or applied, and who may have been discounted at some earlier point due to perceived life constraints. Some may be women who previously downshifted their careers and worked reduced schedules and are now ready to ramp up again. You will need to reach out to your business and network and human resources representatives intentionally to identify women who historically have not been considered qualified candidates.

- Look at ways to bring back women who previously worked for your company or elsewhere and left the workforce for a time. Work with your human resources department to identify and reach out to these women. Some companies call these *returnships* and have even hired or assigned a dedicated coach or peer mentor to help women transition back into the workforce.

- Insist that recruiters provide you with a diverse pool of candidates for every job opening. A regional vice president at Salesforce, a global cloud computing company, shared with me that he believes that his implementation of this practice has been one of the main reasons his team composition is 40% female (uncommon for a tech sales team).

- Have at least two women candidates for consideration for senior level positions or positions traditionally held by men. One is not enough. A study conducted by Stefanie K. Johnson, PhD, David R. Hekman, PhD, and Elsa T. Chan, a doctoral candidate, concluded that if there is only one woman or minority candidate in a pool, there is little to no chance that person will be hired. The odds increase if there is more than one woman or minority candidate in a slate being considered.[9] One way to change deeply ingrained biases is to influence the decision-making environment by the choices you give people.[10]

- Use structured interviews that are based on a fixed, predetermined set of questions rather than unstructured interviews during which interviewers can ask whatever occurs to them. Structured interviews reduce incidences of all types of bias, not just gender bias.

- Check to be sure your "culture fit" questions or assessments aren't gender biased, and that they are not eliminating people who simply are not like the people you already have on board (if your current teams are not diverse).

I spent an afternoon with a group of recruiters who had a lot of open positions and recognized that they were not tapping into the pool of female candidates. When we examined their job postings, they were able to see clearly how the language used discouraged not only women candidates, but also the type of person they really wanted to attract, regardless of gender. For example, almost all their job postings began with the words "under close supervision" (even mid- and higher-level job postings were described this way). This type of language is not appealing to creative, innovative people. Many of the job descriptions listed qualifications and requirements that the people they actually hire rarely meet. These difficult-to-find qualifications were probably deterring women from applying. A widely quoted Hewlett Packard report indicates that women are less likely to apply for opportunities unless they meet 100% of qualifications, believing they will not be hired, whereas men will apply for jobs where they have 60% of the requirements, believing they can learn the rest.[11]

Back to the group of recruiters, when we examined where they went to recruit talent, we learned that they weren't participating in women's networks in their industry. We further identified that when managers and leaders from their company attended industry conferences, they weren't equipped with a list of job openings and were not tasked to identify and connect with talented people who could be candidates.

There may be some of you now wondering why you should have to go to such lengths to recruit and retain women. Simple: diverse teams are more productive, innovative, and make more money. It's never been easy to find top talent, but it's always been worth the effort.

Interact regularly with your female colleagues. Generally speaking, it's easier and more comfortable for people to relate to and work with someone who is like them. In the workplace, that often translates to men working more closely with men and women interacting more frequently with other women. Recently, as

I worked with the employees of a very progressive architecture firm, several architects had an "aha" moment when they realized the potential implications of their customary habit of men eating lunch with other men and women eating lunch together.

To fully leverage the benefits of diversity, interact and collaborate with all your teammates, not only with a select group of them. Intentionally seek out your female colleagues and meet more regularly with them, both formally and informally, as you do with your male colleagues.

To complicate matters, in some cultures the idea of a man and woman meeting together one-on-one is not acceptable. But of course, this is a requirement for people who want to build a professional relationship and work effectively together. There's nothing inherently wrong with a man meeting with a woman at dinner, at a bar, or over drinks. We are professionals and capable of acting professionally. We don't need to shy away from certain places or times. What we need to do is to always act appropriately.

But, if male/female meetings are not an accepted practice in your culture, or if you feel uncomfortable with them, you'll need to find ways to meet with your female coworkers that works for both of you.

Here are a few ideas to try:

- Be very clear and conscious that you are having a business meeting, not a social get-together, by the place you pick to meet and the tone you set.

- Have your meetings in a professional versus social setting.

- If appropriate, broaden in-person meetings to include more people.

- Conduct yourself as if your mother were watching you.

Include women in networking activities, especially ones with clients and executives. Women tell me that they often find themselves a step behind, not "in the know," or left out of important developments and decisions at work. Frequently, they figure out that the reason they don't know what's going on is due to a conversation that took place at a gathering to which they were not invited.

Sure, impromptu gatherings with work colleagues occur. When they do, take a minute to look around the office and think about your female colleagues. Invite them to join you. It's easy enough to send a short text message telling them where your group will be, if you can't immediately locate them.

If you find yourself gathered and all your teammates are not present, postpone in-depth business conversations and decisions until you are all together. You can simply say something like "Let's wait to talk about this until Shonda and Valeria can weigh in."

I understand that male colleagues (and female colleagues) who are friends enjoy getting together as a group. When business topics come up during these gatherings, as they inevitably will, make every effort not to make any decisions, and take it upon yourself to bring your fellow coworkers up to speed as soon as possible.

One of the most important types of networking each of us can do for our careers and business success is to interact with our clients, prospects, and senior managers. Especially commit to include your female colleagues in these types of gatherings.

Give direct and actionable, not vague feedback. At Stanford University, Professor of Sociology and Organizational Behavior Shelley Correll, PhD, and senior researcher and specialist on women's leadership, Caroline Simard, PhD, report: "Our research shows that women are systematically less likely to receive specific, constructive and critical feedback tied to outcomes, both when they receive praise and when the feedback is developmental. In other words, men are offered a clearer picture of what they are doing well and more specific guidance of what is needed to get to the next level."[12]

Set up the women on your team for success. Establish regular meetings with female teammates. Give them the same type of direct feedback you give your male colleagues and staff. Don't be vague or focus solely on generalities like communication or interpersonal skills when you give a woman feedback. Tell her specifically what she needs to know to excel, such as which skills to build and which specific assignments to take on. Table 4.2 shows a few examples.

When you give feedback, don't rely on a woman's self-assessments as the starting point for your assessment. Many women, especially those from cultures with strong social norms about modesty, are reluctant to self-promote and consequently assign themselves lower ratings than they deserve. Managers who rely on these employees's self-appraisals can put women at a disadvantage.[13]

Like my former client, don't fall into the trap of failing to give feedback because you are worried about how the recipient might react.

Table 4.2 **Examples of Direct Constructive Feedback**

Instead of saying...	Try this
I'd like you to be more assertive.	Here are a few things you could do to be more assertive in meetings: Be prepared with your point of view. Jump in to a discussion when other team members are dominating, even if that means occasionally interrupting them. Follow up after the meeting to remind people of their commitments.
Other team members bring in more clients/business than you do.	Here are a few things you could do to bring in more clients/business. Develop expertise in X topic. Attend these types _____ of networking events and connect with these types _____ of prospects.
Please be more helpful.	In the future, please do this _____. Or, stop doing X.

One of the most frequent questions I'm asked by men during presentations I give on this topic is: "What do I do if a woman starts crying when I am giving her feedback?"

Here are my usual answers:

ASSESS your approach. Is your tone calm and constructive, or frustrated and punitive?

ARE you giving forward feedback, saying, "Next time do this," or merely listing everything that's wrong?

ASK the woman how you should interpret her crying.

- Is crying a typical emotional response for her, and would she like you to continue?
- Would she like a minute to collect herself?
- Why is she crying – frustration or anger at herself or you?

BASED on your self-assessment and the woman's responses, decide if you should alter your approach and proceed with the meeting or reschedule for a time when you are both more prepared.

WHATEVER you do, don't obscure the bottom-line message you want to convey. Be direct, factual, and specific.

Sponsor high-potential women. One of the most powerful things that a man (or woman) can professionally do for a woman is to sponsor her.

What is a sponsor? A sponsor is a person with the power, desire, and intention to help a protégé advance in his or her career or business. A sponsor is an advocate and champion. The purpose of sponsorship is not to give advice, such as a mentor would, but to deliberately advocate that someone receive opportunities, promotions, and recognition.

I frequently find that both men and women don't know what a sponsor is, or they misunderstand what a sponsor does. Although leaders claim to understand the role of a sponsor, they confuse being a mentor for being a sponsor or they fail to sponsor women to the extent they do men. See Table 4.3.

Table 4.3 **Differences Between What Mentors and Sponsors Do**

Mentors	Sponsors
Sounding board	Champion
Advise	Advocate
Give their time	Give opportunities
Help a person change	Make change happen
Work privately with their mentees	Work publicly for their protégés
Mentees drive the relationship based on their needs	Sponsors drive the relationship and outcome

Here's an example of sponsorship in the words of Lourdes Lamasney Perez, based on her experience in Spain. "José María Pujol became not only my boss, but also my sponsor. He didn't only help me understand the industry and the market, he gave me visibility within the agency by giving my ideas credit to the head of the agency. It was because of his influence that I was offered a job at Casadevall as a Creative Director. After working with him for a while, he helped me decide to go to Mexico as an expat and a Creative Head for Ogilvy, even though he wanted me to stay in Barcelona as part of his team."

The most successful leaders can spot talent and especially untapped potential. They have the courage to take a chance on employees who may not be completely "ready" for an assignment. An example would be assigning a relatively junior person to a high-profile project, client, or assignment. Adena Friedman, now the CEO of the Nasdaq stock exchange, describes one of her early bosses: "The man I worked for saw me as someone who was an MBA grad. He would give me something to do, and I would go do it, and I would do it well. He never once made me feel at all different or disadvantaged by being a woman. I just got stuff done. When I got my first promotion, I was actually pregnant. For him it was like: "Oh, that's fine. You'll

be gone for three months, and you'll come back."
He really just didn't even factor it into his decision
making. I've had three very important sponsors of
my career, all men. And it's not like they sat there
and had to do a lot to push, push, push me forward. They offered advice when I asked for it, and
they gave me opportunity when they saw it, and
that's all they had to do."[14]

If you are a strong sponsor, high-potential people will
want to work for you. I and many women and men I
know have clearly benefited from being sponsored
throughout our careers.

At most companies, women get less access to senior leaders than their male colleagues. Although
both men and women consider receiving sponsorship from senior leaders essential to their success,
women report having fewer substantive interactions
with senior leaders than their male counterparts do
– a gap that widens as women and men advance.[15]
Your deliberate actions can change this imbalance.

The second issue is that there are very few resources
to guide people on how to be a good sponsor.
Case in point: If you Google the phrase "How to be
a sponsor," you'll get links to thousands of articles
explaining what *you* need to do to get a sponsor, but

none on *being a sponsor*. When I did my own search, I could not find a single article on how to *be* a sponsor.

To remedy that, here are some step-by-step guidelines to get started.

How to Be a Sponsor

Step 1. **Pick**. Identify someone whom you think has high performance, high potential, and ambition. In this case, choose a woman. *Note: if it's unclear to you whether she has career/ business ambitions, ask her. Don't assume she does not. You may have to encourage her to recognize her own potential.*

Step 2. **Plan**. Identify a high-visibility challenging opportunity, role, or assignments that your chosen protégé would excel in and which, if she's successful, would benefit her career/business and your business goals.

Step 3. **Position**. Recommend your protégé for the assignment or give her one of these opportunities.

(continued)

Sponsorship (*continued*)

Step 4. **Prepare**. Talk to your protégé (or have someone talk to her) about the importance of the assignment.

Step 5. **Prevail**. Monitor your protégé's performance during every assignment. Give her or ensure that she receives detailed feedback, advice, and resources to succeed. Keep at it. It will take more than one assignment for her to develop and get to a senior or influential role. Also, she may not have immediate success.

Step 6. **Pave the way**. Introduce and endorse your protégé to influential, powerful people in your organization or industry, including clients. Talk about her, her skills, and why you think she's the right person for an assignment to others.

Step 7. **Protect**. Don't let criticism, mistakes, failures, or naysayers unduly derail her. There's no need to be overly protective or to not allow her to make mistakes or fail. That's how we all learn.

Your role is make sure she's getting direct, actionable feedback and allow space for her to learn from these difficult experiences. If possible, provide her with access to talk to other people who've encountered similar hardships in their career.

Step 8. **Promote**. Advocate for or give raises, promotions, and recognition to your protégé.

Step 9. **Provide**. Invest time, expertise, and money in your protégé. Making financial investments in women entrepreneurs or ventures warrants a more detailed explanation.

If you are not in a role or position to be a sponsor, you can be an ally and/or an advocate for your female colleagues. Being an ally is a critically important role. When you are an ally you are on a woman's side and you find ways to partner with or promote her contributions.

Invest in women-led businesses. Successful business-men – especially male venture capitalists (VCs), corporate executives, and CEOs – have a huge opportunity to make their time, their expertise, their networks, and their capital available to accelerate the growth of women-led businesses. To be fair, there are some male VCs doing exactly that. During a five-year period, Adam Quinton of Lucas Point Ventures invested in 15 companies, 13 of which had at least one female founder. Jeremy Liew, a partner at the prominent Silicon Valley early-stage firm Lightspeed Venture Partners, invested $178 million in companies founded by female entrepreneurs.[16]

And here's an example of a man who both invested capital and sponsored a woman entrepreneur in an unexpected part of the world, Jordan.

When she was 21 years old and recently graduated from university, Tamara Abdel Jaber met successful entrepreneur Khaled Kilani. She shared her desire to start her own business, and he recognized her potential. He made her a promise. If she agreed to work with him for five years and learn every aspect of making a business successful, he would make a financial investment in a business of her own. She did, and he did.

Five years to the date, with Kilani's investment, Tamara launched Palma, a business and IT consulting company. The company has nutured employees and contracts with hundreds of employees. Kilani is the board chair. In 2011, Tamara was named one of the 100 most powerful Arab women, and her company, Palma, was recognized as one of the 30 fastest-growing companies in Jordan.

Between 2010 and 2015, only 10% of global venture dollars, a total of $31.5 billion went to startups with at least one female founder.[17] For one clue about this grave disparity, consider the June 2017 research findings that revealed that both male and female VCs ask women founders different types of question than they ask male founders. Questions to male entrepreneurs focused on potential gains and upsides – in other words, about scaling.[18] Questions to women entrepreneurs were framed on potential loses and downside – in other words, about survival.

The questions asked by VCs impact how the entrepreneurs respond and influence how much funding male-led versus female-led companies receive. This is not only an issue for the female-led firms but can also negatively influence returns for the investors who may have underestimated the challenges that the male entrepreneurs will inevitably encounter and miss the potential opportunities that female entrepreneurs may have.

In another study of *both* male and female government VCs in Sweden, the researchers concluded that with a few exceptions, women were stereotypically described as not having qualities considered important to being an entrepreneur and their credibility, trustworthiness, experience, and knowledge were questioned. Conversely, male entrepreneurs were commonly described as being assertive, innovative, competent, experienced, knowledgeable, and having established networks.[19]

Institutional investors are also starting to take note. Katharine Zaleski, the Cofounder and President of Power to Fly was contacted by two institutional investors, Invesco and Cambridge Associates, inquiring about the professional behavior of male VCs whom they were considering funding.[20]

If you are an investor, ask yourself these questions:

Questions for Investors

DO you have a diversity goal/priority for your VC or investor group?

HAVE you looked at the application process you've defined for entrepreneurs to apply for funding, to ensure that the language and the process do not inadvertently discourage women from applying?

DO you ask the founders of the companies you've invested in about their gender-diversity goals, diversity initiatives, and the number of women and minorities they've hired and promoted into leadership roles?

DO you always describe entrepreneurs, angel investors, and VCs as men?

DO you describe female entrepreneurs differently than you do male entrepreneurs (e.g., "young and promising" [male] versus "young and inexperienced" [female])?

DO you ask female entrepreneurs different questions from the ones you pose to male entrepreneurs?

HOW and how often do you encourage women entrepreneurs to grow their businesses and apply for funding?

If men like Khaled Kilani can make investments in women entrepreneurs in Jordan, men all over the world can do the same. Like successful male high-growth entrepreneurs, high-growth women entrepreneurs need encouragement, mentors, sponsors, connections, and capital from investors to succeed.

Five-Minute Self-Assessment

Answer the following questions. Jot down some notes. Reflect on your responses. Commit to take an action or make a change.

- Do I have the right talent to innovate, anticipate, and produce the high-level results required? What can I do to get the right mix of talent?

- When I look at my professional network, what percent of my contacts are men? Are women?

- How frequently do I professionally interact and network with women?

- Do I invest in women with time and money in the same way I invest in men?

- Do I invest in improving the way men and women work and collaborate together?

- Do I give women the same types of direct feedback and challenging assignments that I give men?

- Do I sponsor an equal number of men and women?

- Which woman can I sponsor and what do I want to advocate for her?

Summary

A disengaged, disinterested, or benign approach to the women on your team will not lead to the business results you are after. A gender-mixed team where both men and women feel valued will better understand customer and market needs, make better decisions, and deliver higher results.

To fully engage women, expand the way you recruit women and the frequency and nature of your interactions with them. Be proactive, listen, make sure they are heard, amplify their contributions, and ensure they have opportunities to excel. Use your power and spend your money on their behalf.

More frequent intentional interactions will make a huge difference to women's success. Sometimes, they will also need a little *ENCOURAGEMENT*.

05

Encourage

Encourage a woman to achieve her potential and ambitions by how you support, recognize, develop, mentor, and prompt her.

ENCOURAGE

What Women Want

- Advice and opportunities

- To be acknowledged for their efforts as well as their results

- Support and encouragement

- To be valued for their demeanor and leadership style

- For their insights and achievements to be more visible

The Problem

According to an analysis of more than 100,000 quantitative and qualitative statements from men and women conducted by Barbara Annis and John Gray, PhD, authors of *Work with Me*, women's top complaint in the workplace is not feeling valued or appreciated.[1]

More times than I care to remember, in conversations with managers and leaders and in succession-planning or talent-development meetings, I have heard leaders make assumptions about a woman's ambitions or her interest and willingness to take on a challenging or international assignment.

I have heard remarks like "She has young children, no way she'd want to do this," "This role requires a lot of hours and travel, and I don't think she'd want to do that," and "She seems happy in her current position." But, the reality is that both men and women are ambitious and seek challenging career advancement opportunities. Here's an example.

Robin Sterneck told me how Ron Pressman, the leader of small group of people sent in by GE to work on a portfolio company, recognized her talent and potential and gave her the right types of career-advancement opportunities. Not long after Robin started working with Ron, "he gave me my first P&L (profit and loss) opportunity. He also actively supported Women's Network efforts throughout GE." An additional detail,

Robin and her husband, a business owner, have four children, who were young at the time. P&L opportunities are critical to the development of leaders, to increased earning and career advancement. The lack of P&L experience is often a determinant limiting factor in a woman's career progression.

A research study in the oil and gas industry conducted by the Boston Consulting Group showed that "women are in fact just as flexible as men, and sometimes even more so. The differences in opinion between men and women about the challenges women face are particularly evident with regard to women's underrepresentation in the senior ranks. On the subject of support, 57% of women said that female employees receive less support for advancement into senior positions than male employees; only 24% of men agreed. About promotion, 56% of women said that women are overlooked for senior positions; only 23% of men agreed."[2]

There has been a great deal of research conducted about whether there's a *leadership ambition gap* among women. Some studies report that women have the same level of ambition as men[3] and others show that women's ambitions change at different stages in their lives and regarding their desire for the most senior roles.[4]

In the recent past, I've coached six different women whose spouses are either stay-at-home dads or the children's primary caregivers. These women were either at the top of their organizations or very intent on getting there. Experience shows that the most important thing to know regarding a woman's ambition is that you cannot make any assumptions. The only way to know is to ask her about her current career aspirations (just as you should ask your male employees), and ask her frequently.

Another factor at play in some women's lack of career advancement can be lower self-confidence. While I hate to acknowledge it, and work very hard to change it, there certainly are some women who are less certain about their ability to take on a challenging assignment or promotion. This is particularly formidable for technology companies. Women underrate themselves in digital acumen and technology skills when asked to score their own effectiveness.[5]

As referenced in the last chapter, it is also not a good idea to rely on women's self-assessments in a performance review. Many companies require employees to assess themselves first on the performance review document, then give it to their manager to include additional information and finalize the review. This practice can put women at a negative starting point because their self-assessment is often worded less favorably than their male colleague's self-evaluation may be framed.

You may find that some of your male employees have similar insecurities. You'll want to encourage them, too.

Unintended Consequences

A female executive shared an experience that occurred when she lived in London.

Executives at her company assumed that there would be no way she would take an international assignment because of her husband's job. She is married to a prominent businessman. When she learned the reason she had not been offered an opportunity, she confronted her manager and told him that it was not up to him or anyone else to decide what she was willing or unwilling to do for her career, nor what her family would or would not do – his job was to offer her opportunities where the company needed her, and she would make her own call.

Recognizing his mistake, he offered her an opportunity in South Africa. She took it.

Future Planning: Don't assume!

SOLUTIONS – WHAT WORKS

At a Glance
Actions You Can Take

Encourage:

- Be a mentor who offers sound advice and support.

- Ensure that women and their contributions are heard.

- Recognize women's efforts as well as their results.

- Recognize women's strengths, potential, and leadership style.

- Provide the types of positively impactful professional development opportunities that lead to career progression.

- Urge women to take challenging or high-profile assignments that have high advancement value.

What One Leader Did

The head of talent and development at a very large regional business shared with me his company's experience in encouraging a high-potential woman not long ago. During the woman's tenure, she repeatedly had to be persuaded to consider, apply for, and take on promotions. Although each time she took a new role, she excelled, the next time she was still unsure if she would be capable of the increased responsibility. As each opportunity presented itself, he and others had to convince her she could do it.

I realize how frustrating it might be to have to repeatedly encourage someone to apply for an opportunity that is in her own best interest. You might be thinking, *it is ridiculous to have to expend that much effort*. But if you value that person's contributions as much as this company did, you'd ask yourself, *what is the price we pay or the results we give up by not earning the best productivity and from not having a gender-diverse team?* and you'd chalk it up to another one of the actions it takes to run a high-performing company.

What You Can Do

Move from assumptions TO action. Instead of assuming, "If women want the opportunities, they will apply," amplify the contributions of women and support, advise, and encourage them to pursue assignments and opportunities. Be persistent!

How?

Proactively mentor women. What is a mentor? A mentor offers feedback and sound advice based on experience and insights. A mentor is both a sounding board and a coach. Mentoring is relational, but it does not have to last forever, nor does it need to be burdensome. Usually, the mentee seeks out the mentor's advice only when she needs it. Still, it's a good idea to remind the women you mentor that you are available to them when they need support or guidance.

One of the leaders I most admire is Esther George, the President and Chief Executive Officer of the Federal Reserve Bank of Kansas City. She has an unparalleled ability to explain the most complex economic and monetary policies and situations in the simplest, clearest terms that everyone can understand. Two other characteristics also distinguish Esther from most other Federal Reserve Bank presidents: she is a woman and not an economist. Esther shared with me that she credits the mentoring she received from Tom Hoenig during her career as key to her advancement and success.

"Tom Hoeing was in a management role as a bank examiner, when I started at the Fed in 1982. From 1982 to 1991, I worked in roles where he was several levels above me, but I had exposure to him through various assignments. In 1991, Tom became president and CEO, and by that time, I had taken on various management roles. In 2001, I was named a division head and began reporting directly to him. Over the next decade, from 2001 to 2011, in that role and eventually when I became the Bank's chief operating officer, I saw firsthand his leadership style and mentoring approach.

"When I think about Tom's role in my professional development, I come back to the confidence that he had in me early in my career and how that encouraged me to have more confidence in myself. Tom is a great teacher, and he would give me assignments that at the time I thought were probably pushing my limits or were even beyond my abilities. But he knew that it was those assignments where I was going to have to work harder and probably make some mistakes that were so important to my development. Like a lot of bosses, Tom would ask my opinion. When you work for someone who is involved in your development, those types of questions can sometimes feel like they only want to see if you know the right answer. But it became apparent pretty quickly that Tom was interested in hearing how other people, including not only me but others as well, thought about issues. That's important and, for me, it really made me think in a more critical way about policy issues, but also on matters where there was no clear answer. In those instances, I think these experiences were very important in helping me develop the skills necessary to formulate my views and present them with a well-supported argument. I also appreciated that while we were involved in a lot of important work and, because of that, sometimes long hours, Tom understood that I had responsibilities outside of work, particularly when my children were young. I can recall situations when I would pick up a child from daycare and bring them back to the office while we completed work on a project. He retired in 2011, and I was named the Bank's president. He remains a mentor to me today."

In a short survey of 35 women from 12 countries, that I conducted, "mentoring" was the most frequent answer to the question about what women appreciated most about their male managers and the colleagues who positively impacted their careers or business.

Other answers included: "He taught me," "He believed in me," "He recognized my strengths and potential," "He shared his knowledge," "He gave me feedback and told me the truth," and "He helped me think about my career plan and direction."

I was heartened by the support and commitment of Yuriy Balkin, who came to one of my speaking engagements in Ukraine in 2017. He returned to see me the next day and waited patiently to talk to me about a female client. He admired her, but felt she needed more confidence and greater business acumen. He wanted to explore ideas with me about resources, support, and coaching that he could provide her. He even followed up and had a call with me to discuss how he could better support her.

I've had many male mentors over my career and have also seen and read about many, many men who are formal mentors to women through company programs and various platforms like the Cartier Women's Initiative, Cherie Blair Foundation, Techstars, and Endeavor, to name just a few.

Ensure that women and their contributions are heard and acknowledged. One of the most frequent universal complaints and frustrations of women around the world is how they are regularly interrupted in meetings.[6] They also tell me how many times what they say in a meeting is not acknowledged, and yet will be repeated a few minutes later by a man. The man's statement will be received as if everyone had just heard it for the first time. By the way, young people or less experienced people are also often interrupted and overlooked. A former U.S. Marine and graduate of two Ivy League universities shared with me how, as the youngest member and most junior member of his team, his contributions are often overlooked. I'm not sure how you overlook a former marine!

I've even heard Indra Nooyi, CEO of PepsiCo, talk about how this used to happen to her before she became CEO. She shared that finally, one day, so frustrated that her ideas were not heard until a male colleague presented them, she stopped a meeting and told everyone to hold on, that she was going to say something to one of her male colleagues so he could share it with them. That was the last time she was ignored.

Typically, men don't realize they do this. When I brought up the phenomenon at a session with senior corporate executives, one of them asked everyone at the meeting, "Really, do we do this?" All the women in the room groaned loudly in response.

To stop this widespread practice, amplify women's contributions. There are four primary ways to do so: in meetings, by the way you introduce women, online, and through your support and encouragements. Here are a few concrete techniques. These techniques will also be greatly appreciated by and help you get input from introverts and anyone else on your team who is quieter, younger, more junior, or who comes from a culture where boldly asserting an opinion is not common or who is reluctant to speak.

In meetings, consider ways to amplify the voices of women or anyone else whose input is not regularly heard or hasn't been appropriately considered, such as new team members or junior staff.

- When a woman makes an important point, verbally acknowledge and point out the importance of what she said by saying things like: "Aisha just made an important point. That was really helpful, did everyone key in on what Joann said? What Fernanda just said made me think about this issue in a new way."

- If a woman is interrupted, either stop the interrupter or circle back around to her after the interruption is over. One way to stop the interrupter is to say something like "Sergio, Julia hasn't finished her thought yet. After she's done, we'll come right back to you." Or after the interrupter is done speaking, you can say, "Susanna, it sounded like you had more to say, please continue." Or you can do something like what a few teams at the collaboration software development company Atlassian do. They have rubber chickens in meeting rooms that people can "squeak" when someone has taken up too much air time or interrupts a colleague.[7]

- If a man makes a point or suggestion that a woman has already made, say, "Yes, thanks Joe, Maria brought that up earlier." Or "Thank you for bringing Sue's good idea back up."

- Stop men from condescendingly explaining something to a woman or insisting that they know more about a subject than she does, when she is clearly knowledgeable or experienced in the subject area. This practice of silencing or discrediting a woman or hijacking her opportunity to speak is so common that it has a name. Women call it *mansplaining*. Personally, I don't like this mash-up, as I try to avoid using derogatory terms to refer to anyone's behavior. We don't need to label the behavior, we just need to stop it from happening.

- If women (or others at the meeting) don't speak up in a meeting that you are in, ask them if they have anything they'd like to add.

- When a woman is speaking, look directly at her. Give her your undivided attention and lean forward as you listen. Don't look off to the side, as men often do when talking with another man, or think of what you may want to say next. This is a good listening technique to use, regardless of who is speaking.

- If a woman is providing details that you don't think are necessary, be patient. Keep listening. (Also, try doing this when your wife/girlfriend is talking to you!) You might learn something you didn't know. Your goal is to absorb what she is saying, not to find an opening to rebut or interrupt her. When she's done, then it's yours or someone else's turn. (If you think she consistently provides too much detail in her communications, give her that feedback and some tips to improve in a separate session with her.)

- Time speakers. Compare the speaking times of the woman and men in your meetings by informally timing and adding up conversation durations. (Note: some conference calling services automatically provide you with a summary of participant talking times.)

- Remind the women you work with (I frequently do so) to speak up and take the risk of offering their perspectives, and to stop people from them interrupting them.

Here in her own words is Aline Clavellina's positive experience with her manager. "At an earlier stage in my career, my manager frequently would ask me to come by his office after our monthly manager meetings to explain to him in more detail my point of view, or a decision I had made. Initially, I did not understand why he regularly had this extra meeting with me. I asked myself if I wasn't being clear enough, and I wondered if he was doing the same with the rest of my male colleagues. The bright side was that I had more time to discuss and present my point of view with him. But I continued to feel that I was being treated somehow differently ... and that worried me. Did I have communication problems? Was I not assertive enough or an ineffective decision-maker?

"After a while, I was promoted. Before starting my new assignment, I went to thank my previous manager and say goodbye. I could not resist asking him why he had always asked me to further explain myself. He smiled, and kindly explained: 'You are an extremely fast thinker. Most of the time you arrive at a conclusion in half the time it takes others to follow your track. At the beginning, I was unclear about the rationale behind your thinking. But, before assuming your decision-making process was not correct, I decided to only assume that your approach was different. My obligation is to understand the way you see things. I am a father of a woman who always surprises me with her different perspective of things, compared to her brother and to my own way of thinking ... so, instead of arriving at premature conclusions, I decided to understand you better. So, I started meeting with you after our monthly meetings to understand how you'd arrived at your conclusions. I confirmed then, that your thinking process was different and faster than the rest of ours. That's what made me recommend you for a promotion. Now, I will go to your next manager, and explain to him how he should pay attention to your perspectives, insights, and decisions so he can benefit from them as I have."

Make women and their insights, achievements, and aspirations more visible.

- Regularly communicate female colleague's contributions, leadership, and results to your colleagues, clients, and senior leaders.

- When you are at a networking event or a meeting with clients or senior executives, introduce your female colleague by her recent accomplishments, expertise, title, or ambitions. For instance, say: "I'd like you to meet Sandra, she's our resident expert on X and she recently solved one of our client's biggest problems."

- Make high-performing women more visible inside your organization and externally in the marketplace by making them the lead person for an important initiative, sharing their accomplishments, and publicly recognizing their performance. Seeing female role models is encouraging and motivating to other women, especially young women, and a factor they consider when deciding where to work.

- Share articles or insights from your female colleagues online and through social media. Include praise or support for their ideas.

Encourage women to accept credit for their success and to make their aspirations known.

- Encourage women you know and work with to accept credit for their accomplishments. For example, when you compliment a woman for her results, don't accept her saying, "It was nothing."

- Urge women to communicate their aspirations and achievements. This is one of the most valuable actions women can take to advance themselves.

Recognize women's efforts as well as their results. There are differences between how men and women prefer to be acknowledged for their contributions. Based on the Annis – Gray diagnostic survey, we know that men feel appreciated when they are acknowledged and rewarded for producing a result. By contrast, women feel appreciated when both the challenges they encountered and their efforts are acknowledged along with recognition of their actual results.[8] When I bring up this topic up at my speaking events, men in attendance inevitably tell me that many men also want to be recognized for both their results and their efforts. So, as with most of the other practices contained in this book, these are good actions for managers and peers when working with both women and men.

Provide impactful professional development opportunities. Don't rely solely on training to develop women. The least effective way to develop leadership in anyone is through training. Yet, many companies rely almost exclusively on women's leadership development training programs as their vehicle to promote women leaders.

The most effective way you can support a woman with leadership potential is to give her challenging assignments; take her out of staff positions and put her into an operating line, a revenue, or a profit-and-loss position; and involve her in strategic business decision-making.

Consciously and deliberately think about the women on your team. Don't overlook women because you spend more time with the men in your office or because the men are more visible, work longer hours in the office, or ask for opportunities more frequently.

Start by identifying a woman's strengths and interests. Determine where in your business the greatest need and opportunities for her skill set exists. Advocate for her to have (or give her) those opportunities.

Encourage women's advancement. Tell women when you consider them ready for challenging opportunities or assignments. Say something like: "You are ready for this, go ahead and apply." Be persistent; you may have to urge her a few times.

A female leader at Google shared with me that she had an opportunity to be considered for a promotion. While she had consistently been a top performer, she didn't feel that her current results warranted the consideration. She expressed her hesitation to her manager, also sharing that she was "too busy" to go through the promotion consideration process. Her manager refused to accept her self-imposed limitations by reminding her of her accomplishments and telling her that all the paperwork would be taken care of.

It is not solely your responsibility to make opportunities available for women who work with you; they are equally responsible. But you are critical in opening doors to their future advancement.

Five-Minute Self-Assessment

Answer the following questions. Jot down some notes. Reflect on your responses. Commit to take an action or make a change.

- Do I think differently about the ambitions of my male and female teammates or clients?

- Have I made assumptions about the ambitions of my female teammates and their interest in opportunities?

- Do I promote my female colleagues, their accomplishments, and their perspectives to the same extent and frequency as I do for men? Where and when could I do so more consistently?

- What is the ratio of male to female input at meetings I hold or attend?

- Which women do I mentor? How regularly and frequently? How does that compare with the mentoring I provide men?

- Which women could I encourage?

- Have I developed high-potential women not only through training or conferences but also by giving them challenging assignments?

Summary

Women (like men) sometimes need a little encouragement. They need to feel that their managers believe in them and have their best interests at heart. Sometimes they need to be told more than once that they are capable. They value and want your advice and support.

Women also want you to *ENGAGE*.

06

Engage

Engage in work-life programs, "work-keeping" tasks, and women's networks and initiatives.

ENGAGE

What Women Want

- Acknowledgment and empathy for their work-life demands

- Shared labor versus a division of labor

- Support for women's initiatives and networks

The Problem

According to research from McKinsey & Company, fewer men than women acknowledge the challenges female employees face at work.[1] A more complete understanding would help managers better structure work environments and demands, as well as increase retention of female employees.

Women tell me that they constantly must explain, justify, apologize, and ask permission for their work-life demands and priorities. They wish that their managers would keep their life constraints in mind, so they wouldn't need to remind them continually.

On the other hand, they also say that some managers assume that all family responsibilities are theirs even though many men in workplaces – and increasingly so among millennial men – now share in home and family duties.

Everybody benefits from managers who are attuned to people's need to balance work and life.

Further, in office environments, it's common to see women handle what are euphemistically referred to as *work-keeping* or *office-keeping* tasks. Similar in nature to housekeeping chores, these tasks include taking notes at meetings, ordering refreshments, planning meetings or events, sending out invitations to events, and clearing up a room after a meeting. Unless it's part of a particular woman's job responsibilities to do this type of work, if you default to her or assign her work-keeping tasks, they will interfere with her ability to get her real work done.

In the recent past, many companies have put in place women's networks or initiatives. While these are valued and appreciated by most women and have been helpful to many women's careers, they are often underfunded and treated as side activities or viewed as "We've checked off that box. See, we do value women in our organization and want them to succeed" types of initiatives. These networks rarely have regular activities that include the deep and real participation of senior executives, men, or clients, and therefore an unintended consequence is that women have weaker networks with influential or powerful people in them.

In a survey of 17,500 employees and interviews with 200 executives in 21 countries, 96% of respondents reported progress when men were involved in company gender-diversity initiatives, compared to 30% when men were not involved.[2]

You can develop a better understanding of the challenges women face at home and work by engaging: listening, remembering, not assuming, and participating.

Unintended Consequences

I coached a team of four men and one woman to prepare them to give a very important presentation. They worked hard at developing the presentation, getting their slides created and practicing. During all our rehearsals, the team members advanced the slides pertaining to their own portions of the presentation. I was with them right up until a few minutes before the presentation started.

As I walked out of the room and with no time to stop her, I heard the woman say, "I can advance everyone's slides for them."

"Great, thanks," the three men responded.

Yes, I realize that the woman put herself in this unfortunate and unnecessary work-keeping role, and that by doing so she diminished herself in the eyes of the senior executive audience. But the men in the room should not have let her take on that administrative task alone. The point here is not that they should have stopped her because she was a woman, but that as coworkers, we should have each other's backs and not allow anyone on our team to diminish another's stature.

I spoke firmly to the woman in our next coaching session about how her actions undermined her position and also explained the consequences to her male colleagues.

Future Planning: Figure out a way for work-keeping tasks to be rotated among everyone on the team.

SOLUTIONS – WHAT WORKS

At a Glance
Actions You Can Take

Engage in:

- Time off or a flexible work schedule to attend to personal priorities in your life

- Life/family benefits offered by your company

- Work-keeping tasks, and also ensure that such tasks are equally distributed among the men and women on your team

- Women's initiatives and with companies that are supportive of women

What One Manager Did

I participated on a panel at TEDWomen in October 2016 sponsored by the global design, engineering, and planning firm Arup. The session was structured like a focus group with attendees invited to provide input on what should be considered when designing a city that would work well for women.

The most senior Arup representative in the room was Chris Luebkeman, Global Director of Foresight, Research, and Innovation. Luebkeman was the best example of an executive doing work-keeping that I have ever seen. He stayed mostly in the back of the room, passed out handouts, collected information, and attended to most of the administrative tasks of the session. Francesca Birks, a member of his team, ran the meeting. He did not try to upstage her in any way, and she was clearly the person at the front of the room and in charge.

Watching Luebkeman, I was struck by several things: How the role he took elevated Francesca's stature, how by taking on the administrative tasks, he was privy to the attendees' reactions in a way most executives rarely are, and how he set an example and validated the importance of every task. Through his actions, Luebkeman demonstrated strategic leadership.

What You Can Do

Move from a disinterested approach to work/life obligations and benefits TO making a conscious effort to remember your teammates' personal priorities and disclose your own.

Move from a disengaged approach to workplace tasks and women's initiatives TO an active and engaged approach.

Move from viewing your own life in a two-dimensional way, with work on one side and life on the other. Your career or business does not have to define you.

How?

Keep your teammates' life and family obligations and important outside interests in mind. Listen when they tell you about schedule constraints. Don't make them have to remind you every time you schedule something that conflicts with their responsibilities. If at all possible, provide them with the flexibility they need to take care of their top priorities, and at a minimum, don't create additional hardships for them.

Prioritize and be transparent with your own life/ family obligations. If you have to leave to pick up your child, go to a family activity, or take your mother to the doctor, don't hide why you are leaving. Robert Rietbork, the chief executive of PepsiCo Australia and New Zealand calls it "leaving loudly."[3] The idea is that if leaders disclose when they are leaving for personal reasons, they set an example that it's okay to do so and reduce the perception that women need more flexibility or exclusively attend to family obligations.

When men equally disclose and take on their life obligations, then more people and senior leaders will realize that increasingly men, and not only women, have these demands placed on their time. You too are entitled to a full life. You too can set boundaries on your work and build a full and complete life for yourself. There's no need to hide your family obligations by, for example, saying you have an appointment when you are going to pick up your child. Your example will help reduce the stigma many working mothers face and also help the men on your team who want more flexibility in their lives.

Take advantage of family benefits provided by your employer. If you take advantage of benefits like paternity leave or bereavement leave and your colleagues know about it, then these types of benefits will become more acceptable and seen as employee versus "women's" benefits. Your loved ones and children (if or when you have them) want you to be present in their lives. If you start early in your career to prioritize your life and interests outside work in the same ways you prioritize work, you will reap the fulfillment of an integrated life. If more men participate in benefits like parental leave policies, they will also reduce the likelihood that men who do so are viewed as being on the "daddy-track."

Businesses who understand and accommodate the increase in dual-career families and shared home/

family workloads between women and men, will not only be able to retain more women, they will also be able to keep high-performing men who value their family relationships as much as they value their careers.

Take on work-keeping tasks in all types of meetings, like Chris Luebkeman did. By doing so, you convey how every task is important to the team's success and that no one is above taking any responsibility. Do the same thing at home, and take on home and family responsibilities. You will make a huge difference in the lives of your family.

Ensure that work-keeping tasks on your team are rotated equally among men and women. If the women on your team persist in volunteering, just thank them for offering and say something like, "Lee, you haven't taken notes in a while, thanks for recording our team's agreements today." Don't accept excuses from a male colleague like: "I am not good at note-taking" or "Rosemary is better at planning and follow-up than I am." Note-taking is an important business practice. It's an opportunity to improve listening skills, learn how to summarize discussion, and make connections between deliverables. You and everyone on your team can benefit from honing this skill and using it in meetings with clients, as well as at many other types of meetings.

Champion, lead, and actively participate in important gender initiatives. When you do so, don't be just a figurehead. Make your involvement deep, substantive, and a priority.

I worked for a couple of days with Kuros Ghaffari, who is part of Cultural Affairs in the U.S. State Department. Each time he introduced me, regardless of the setting, he made it a point to talk about my work in equipping men, managers, and leaders to work more effectively with women and how achieving gender parity requires the full support and actions of men.

- As appropriate, attend networking events that your company's women's affiliate group plans. Broaden your connections with women colleagues.

- Invite and encourage male colleagues to also participate.

- Recommend or, if you can, ensure that your company's women's leadership or networking initiatives regularly include interactions with clients and male leaders.

- If you have authority or oversight for gender initiatives, ensure they are adequately funded, valued, and prioritized to make a real impact and not viewed as marginal or obligatory.

Two men I know who live in parts of the world known to be among the most difficult for women have shown remarkable leadership in engaging on behalf of women. The first man, 30-year-old Khalid Alkhudair gave up his job as an auditor at KPMG to found Glowork, a recruiting company for Saudi women. According to Alkhudair, Glowork has helped more than 26,000 women find jobs in Saudi Arabia, and many others have benefited from access to the firm's advice and career fairs.[4]

In addition to his job as the Founder and Creative Director of 4M Designers, a creative digital agency, the second man, Abdul Muizz, founded HerCareer.pk and HerFloor. HerCareer.pk was Pakistan's first online career community of women and connects women to jobs and mentors in Pakistan. Today, the site has more than 67,000 registered women.[5] (Full disclosure, I am one of the mentors.)

I'm not suggesting or advocating that you give up your job or do something as significant as Alkhudair or Muizz did. But if they could do what they did in Saudi Arabia and Pakistan, consider the impact that you could have in Silicon Valley, New York City, London, Sydney, or Tel Aviv if you got involved in programs and initiatives at your company or in your community.

Five-Minute Self-Assessment

Answer the following questions. Jot down some notes. Reflect on your responses. Commit to take an action or make a change.

- Do I know my teammates' primary or important life/family obligations that can be impacted by work demands (for example, taking or picking up children, caring of a family member, or of a pet, or coaching a team)? Try to list them by person, and then check back with each team member to see if you've accurately identified them.

- When was the last time I was transparent about my own family/life obligations?

- What behaviors have I demonstrated lately that sent the right messages about work/life balance? What have I said or done that sent the wrong messages on the importance of both life and livelihood?

- Do we share work-keeping tasks equally among all team members?

- What gender initiatives am I involved in or would I like to participate in?

Summary

Life and family obligations and gender initiatives are not the sole purview of women. Know and make every attempt to honor the primary responsibilities that your teammates have at home. Be open about your own obligations and take advantage of the employee benefits offered to you. Share responsibility for keeping the office and team functioning well. Lead and support gender initiatives. Your involvement will be greatly appreciated and go a long way to making them a success.

Conclusion

I know I've thrown a lot at you. But it's incredibly important, and it's no more than you can handle. It boils down to this: Be more aware and attuned to the needs of women, and work deliberately to include and advance them. Doing so will make a positive difference for them, for you, and for all of us.

Go from an automatic, gut-reaction management approach TO a reflective, conscious one where you intentionally focus on engaging and elevating women. When you do so, you will elevate them and yourself and improve your business results, society, and the economy.

Here's an example of WE 4.0 in action.

How WE 4.0 Works

I coached a woman who had unrealized potential and ambitions. She has the technical expertise her company values and needs to innovate and build relationships with clients and satisfy their needs. But to her own frustration, and her management's, she was grossly underutilized.

The solution, as it usually is, was two-sided.

My client was both doing and not doing several things that were stalling her advancement. A few of her shortcomings: She did not delegate work to the people she managed. Consequently, she was overworked, stressed, and not contributing at a strategic level. She rarely said anything in meetings because she felt that the men on her team (she was the only woman) spoke too fast, and she could not get a word in edgewise. She also believed that before she could say anything, she needed to be 100% prepared and that her idea needed to be fully thought out. Further, outside of her own team, she was not visible in her company, and she had not shared her ambitions with anyone.

Now for the management and company side of the equation. To his credit, her manager saw her potential, but he was frustrated with her. One of the things he shared with me was how unassertive it seemed to him when she would raise her hand if she wanted to say something in a meeting. Also, to their credit, the HR department had recognized her talents and included her in the company's leadership development program. But still she was not advancing.

For the company and her manager to get the full benefit of her expertise and for my client to get the promotion she dearly wanted, we all had to work together. For several months, my client and I worked together on ways she could more readily share her strategic insights, as well as on delegation, self-promotion, networking, and techniques to interject her perspectives. She practiced and learned how to find openings in fast conversations among her male colleagues. We visualized jumping into a conversation in the same way one looks for spaces between cars when merging onto a highway. She began providing input and ideas even if they weren't fully developed. She stopped raising her hand.

Her manager began to specifically call on her in meetings. He no longer accepted her "I'm not sure I'm ready to weigh in" objections. He stopped her male coworkers' interruptions. He also amplified her ideas in meetings he held and around the company, always giving her credit for her insights. He became her sponsor and advocated that the company CEO select her for a major corporate transformational project that the CEO was leading. He put her on one of the company's most important client accounts. The woman took that opportunity and made some significant contributions that improved both the working relationship with and profitability from this client.

It took changes in both the woman and her manager to change her trajectory and contributions. Three years later, she's in the job she wanted to be in: a senior position in the company. (There were a series of job moves prior to this ultimately desired promotion.) The company has also benefited from her deep technical expertise in product innovation and increased its business with one of their most important strategic clients.

You are the Integral Part of the WE Solution

It's widely acknowledged that men still hold most of the power in the world. But do you realize how powerful YOU personally are?

As I explained in the Introduction, the WE 4.0 actions are individual, not institutional. You don't have to wait on anyone else or your company to implement anything before you start adopting them. People like you all around the world are making these types of changes and succeeding in transforming themselves, their careers, their businesses, and the careers of women. You don't need a program, an initiative, or a pledge.

What you feel and think about this topic matters. But what's most important is what you do about it. Doing is what will change the world.

Pick a place to start. Identify one thing to say or do differently this week. Start there. If all you can do right now is to have a conversation with your son about how he interacts with girls and women, then do that. Think about the way you talk to your daughter. If the most frequent type of advice you give her is about being careful or marrying a man who can provide for her, switch and encourage her to take calculated challenges and find ways to provide for herself with or without the right partner. If you've identified one thing you can do to make your team environment more inclusive, do that. If you can recognize a female colleague's contributions, do that. Commit to daily and consistent action.

I know that taking WE 4.0 actions comes with risk. But what's the risk of not taking them? When you consistently take WE 4.0 actions, you will improve your own career trajectory and business results.

Here's what it's been like for a few of the men Darcy Howe has worked with. "Jim, my manager at the time, chose me as his candidate to start a new ultra-high-net-worth group. Not because I had the largest practice, but because he saw that I knew how to serve the ultra-wealthy families. I believe there were three woman-led teams out of 30 teams that were chosen. This new type of work elevated both Jim's visibility and stature, as well as mine. I was given a coveted spot in this new special division, and Jim went on to a national job for the firm." Of course, there was much more involved beyond this one accomplishment that led to both Darcy and Jim's success, including a track record of sustained results, hard work, and expertise to name just a few.

Darcy went on to grow her group at Merrill Lynch and then joined forces with a male colleague, a different Jim, to grow their practice. They grew it into one of the most successful teams, each bringing their best strengths to the business. Darcy's were building relationships with family members of all generations and really understanding their life and financial goals. Jim's were his financial acumen. When Darcy retired from Merrill Lynch/Bank of America, Jim and new partners bought out her share of what had grown into a very successful business. Today, Darcy runs a venture fund. She has thus far funded 15 companies led by men, connected every one of them to business people she's built relationships with over her career, and coached and mentored each of them to improve their odds for their success, the investor's success, Kansas City's success, and her own.

When you work together with women, you will increase your success, drive economic growth, and improve society. You will improve the lives of the women you interact with, including the lives of your coworkers, your clients, your daughter(s), your wife, your sister(s), and your mother.

You will also improve your own life and the lives of men and boys.

You can choose to see these actions as a path to a better, more equitable world or not – that's up to you. But if you use these methods, then we will all benefit.

WE 4.0 at a Glance

Figure C.1 is a recap of what women want and the corresponding WE 4.0 actions for you to use as a reference tool before meetings, during meetings, when recruiting, and in your interactions with women. Refer to it regularly to stay on track. You can also use the checklist that follows (Figure C.2) to see if you've taken the most important steps needed to recruit, retain, and advance women.

Figure C.1 **WE 4.0 at a Glance**

Women Want: →	Your Actions
- A level playing field - To be valued and respected - No discrimination or sexual harassment - To be judged on their performance (output and results), not on their presence (hours) in the office	**Eliminate:** ○ Workplace practices that disproportionately and adversely impact women ○ Discrimination, bias, and microaggressions toward women ○ Any gender-related wage gaps
- To be equally considered for challenging high-profile opportunities and advancement - To be included in formal and informal networking - To be given direct feedback - To have access to senior leaders - To be sponsored in addition to being mentored	**Expand:** ○ Where and how you recruit women ○ The number of female candidates you consider for jobs and opportunities ○ Intentional, regular interactions with female teammates ○ Women offered the same type of direct feedback and challenging assignments offered to male teammates ○ Sponsor high-performing, high-potential women

(continued)

WE 4.0 At a Glance *continued*

Women Want: →	Your Actions
<ul><li>Advice and opportunities</li><li>To be acknowledged for their efforts as well as their results</li><li>Support and encouragement</li><li>To be valued for their demeanor and leadership style</li><li>Their insights and achievements to be more visible</li></ul>	**Encourage:** <ul><li>Be a mentor who offers sound advice and support.</li><li>Amplify women's input and perspectives.</li><li>Recognize women's efforts as well as their results.</li><li>Don't take a woman's self-assessment at face value. Dig in to be sure she has not underrated herself.</li><li>Recognize women's strengths and potential and leadership styles.</li><li>Provide challenging assignments and impactful professional development</li><li>Prompt advancement</li></ul>

(continued)

WE 4.0 At a Glance *continued*

Women Want: →	Your Actions
– Acknowledgment and empathy for their work-life demands – Shared labor versus a division of labor – Support for their initiatives	**Engage:** o Keep your teammates' life/family obligations in mind o Be transparent with your own life/family obligations o Take advantage of family benefits provided by your employer o Personally take on work-keeping tasks and ensure that they are equally distributed among the men and women on your team o Actively participate or lead initiatives that support women

WE 4.0 Checklist

In his bestselling book *The Checklist Manifesto* (Henry Holt and Company, 2009), author, surgeon, and public health researcher, Atul Gawande illustrates how simple checklists increase success in the most complex situations like surgery or an airplane flight. He explains that two of the most common reasons for failure are ignorance (we simply do not know what to do) and ineptitude (we don't apply the knowledge we have consistently and correctly), and that these can be reduced by having a checklist.

I put together the following checklist to increase your and your team's success in recruiting, retaining, and advancing women. If you can check off each of these items, you are in good shape. Add others you think are important and helpful.

Figure C.2 **We 4.0 Checklist**

Eliminate

- ☐ Workplace practices are not negatively impacting any group.
- ☐ Inappropriate comments, sexual harassment, or misconduct are addressed and not tolerated.
- ☐ No gender gap in compensation.

Expand

- ☐ Job ads and descriptions are reviewed.
- ☐ Diverse candidate pool is required.
- ☐ Interview process includes diverse interviewers and diverse decision makers.
- ☐ Regularly scheduled meetings and interactions with women are as frequent as those with men.

Encourage

- ☐ Women are sponsored and have same access to executive leaders as men.
- ☐ Processes are in place for women to be offered same types of challenging and developmental opportunities as men.
- ☐ Gender-equal feedback processes are in place and women are provided with direct, detailed feedback.
- ☐ Women have strong mentors.
- ☐ Women's accomplishments are recognized and visible.
- ☐ High-performing women are promoted at same rates as male colleagues.

Engage

- ☐ Women's initiatives have male leader sponsorship and engagement.
- ☐ Men regularly participate in gender initiatives.
- ☐ Work/office-keeping is equally shared by male and female colleagues.

Acknowledgments

This book is the result of deep collaboration and support among men and women.

Unlike the challenges I had writing my first book, *Undeterred: The Six Success Habits of Women in Emerging Economies*, the first draft of this book flowed right out of me. That was the easy part. But transforming a manuscript into a book happens only through the combined efforts of many engaged readers and publishing experts.

Men and women on four continents (you know who you are) graciously consented to share their workplace experience. You brought this book to life. Seven men, representing my target readers, kindly agreed to serve as my beta-readers. David Aycock, Samer Habiby, Paul MacMillan, Dave Pazgan, John Power, Brandon Shackelford, and my husband, Lance (he had no choice) gave me invaluable feedback, insights, and suggestions. In particular, Paul spent hours with me, catching a hugely critical missing perspective and challenging me over and over again to engage with and appeal to readers on multiple levels.

Next came the voices of women to frame, position, and encourage my writing. Jensen Power offered a valuable initial review, followed by multiple read-throughs and recommendations by my colleague and dear friend, Erin Risner, doing what she and I always refer to as her "magic." My editor, Stephanie Gunning, expertly brought the manuscript into shape and worked with me on my book proposal. Throughout the many months, my dearest friends—Darcy Howe, Diane Power, and Joann Schwarberg—listened to my highs and lows and supported me every step of the way.

Then came what I thought would be the hardest part: finding the right publisher. And, although it took a few months and some initial rejection, the breakthrough came by way of a bond built between a woman and a man based on their shared philosophy of helping others. Lesa Mitchell, managing director at Techstars, calls their method "Give First, Always." She introduced me and my book to Brad Feld, cofounder of Techstars and managing director of Foundry Group, who has written many books. Brad graciously agreed to introduce me to Bill Falloon, his executive editor at John Wiley & Sons.

From the moment Bill and I connected, I felt that we were in sync. I felt heard and understood by him – that he got me, my book, and the impact I hope to make. Through his thoughtful feedback and edits, Bill guided me to further strengthen the book. He went to bat for me at Wiley, and he willingly reached out to his hard-earned client network on my behalf. Along with Bill, the rest of my team at Wiley, Mike Henton, Purvi Patel, and Susan Cerra, also caringly weighed in with their expertise and shepherded the manuscript through the process of becoming a book. At one point, while on a speaking tour, I panicked when I learned about some of the technical requirements for submitting the final manuscript. Charlotte Cline-Smith swooped in and handled these seamlessly for me. The tedious but critical task of proofing fell largely to Steff Hedenkamp. She caught so many things I never would have seen and added the final polish the book needed.

I boldly reached out to a few experts and thought leaders, all of whom I greatly admire, but had no prior connection with most of them, to ask if they would consider reviewing my book. To a person, they got back to me and agreed.

I am especially grateful to Dominic Barton, managing partner at McKinsey & Company, for providing important context and capturing all the nuances in *WE* in his heartfelt foreword and for his tireless leadership in striving to make a truly equitable workplace a reality.

Throughout the whole process I've been supported, challenged, and encouraged by all these people and many more, and most of all by my husband, Lance. I am grateful to each of you for your involvement, expertise, and love. *WE* did it together.

Notes

Introduction

1. "Navigating Disruption without Gender Diversity?" Ernst & Young, Women in Industry, www.ey.com/gl/en/issues/business-environment/ey-women-in-industry (accessed 21 July 2017).

2. World Economic Forum, executive summary, "The Industry Gender Gap: Women and Work in the Fourth Industrial Revolution," January 2016, www3.weforum.org/docs/WEF_FOJ_Executive_Summary_GenderGap.pdf.

3. Dominic Barton, "It's Time for Companies to Try a New Gender-Equality Playbook," *Wall Street Journal*, 27 September 2016, www.wsj.com/articles/its-time-for-companies-to-try-a-new-gender-equality-playbook-1474963861.

4. Dana Kanze, Laura Huang, Mark A. Conley, and E. Tory Higgins, "Male and Female Entrepreneurs

Get Asked Different Questions by VCs – and It Affects How Much Funding They Get," *Harvard Business Review,* 27 June 2017, https://hbr.org/2017/06/male-and-female-entrepreneurs-get-asked-different-questions-by-vcs-and-it-affects-how-much-funding-they-get.

5. Barton, "It's Time for Companies to Try a New Gender-Equality Playbook."

6. Kathleen L. McGinn, Mayra Ruiz Castro, and Elizabeth Long Lingo, "Children Benefit from Having a Working Mom," Harvard Business School, 15 May 2015, www.hbs.edu/news/articles/Pages/mcginn-working-mom.aspx.

7. "The Global Gender Gap Report 2017," World Economic Council, 2 November 2017, www3.weforum.org/docs/WEF_GGGR_2017.pdf.

8. Barton, "It's Time for Companies to Try a New Gender-Equality Playbook."

9. Rhymer Rigby, "Women Need to Encourage Male Colleagues Who Try to Help Them," *Financial Times*, 14 September 2015, www.ft.com/content/8ac17d88-55a3-11e5-9846-de406ccb37f2.

10. Louann Brizendine, as cited by Women's Sport and Fitness Foundation/Sports Coach UK, "Female Psychology and Considerations for

Coaching Practice," WomeninSport.com, April 2015, www.womeninsport.org/wp-content/uploads/2015/04/Female-Psychology-and-Considerations-for-Coaching-Practice.pdf?938151.

11. Heidi Grant Halvorson and David Rock, "Beyond Bias: Neuroscience Research Shows How New Organizational Practice Can Shift Ingrained Thinking," *Strategy + Business*, 13 July 2015, www.strategybusiness.com/article/00345?gko=d11ee&utm_source=itw&utm_medium=20170406&utm_campaign=resp.

Chapter 1: Why Care About Gender Balance at Work?

1. Mike Gamson, "I Care About Diversity Because Diverse Teams Win," LinkedIn.com, 9 November 2015, www.linkedin.com/pulse/i-care-diversity-because-diverse-teams-win-mike-gamson.

2. Muhtar Kent, "Statistics on the Purchasing Power of Women," GirlPowerMarketing.com, October 2010, https://girlpowermarketing.com/statistics-purchasing-power-women.

3. Julia West, "The Difference Between Coaching Boys and Girls ...," *Female Coaching Network*, 24 November 2015, https://femalecoachingnetwork.com/2015/11/24/the-difference-between-coaching-boys-and-girls.

4. Wade Gilbert, "Coaching Males/Coaching Females," Human Kinetics Coach Education Center, 3 March 2016, www.asep.com/news/ShowArticle.cfm?ID=260.

5. Rhymer Rigby, "Women Need to Encourage Male Colleagues Who Try to Help Them," *Financial Times*, 15 September 2015, www.ft.com/content/8ac17d88-55a3-11e5-9846-de406ccb37f2.

6. Adam Quinton, "Want to fix gender inequality at work? Start by asking the right question," *Cartier Women's Initiative Awards*, 15 May 2018, www.cartierwomensinitiative.com/news/want-fix-gender-inequality-work-start-asking-right-question.

7. Jenny Anderson, "Huge Study Finds That Companies with More Women Leaders Are More Profitable," *Quartz*, 8 February 2016, https://qz.com/612086/huge-study-find-that-companies-with-more-women-leaders-are-more-profitable.

8. Christopher Mims, "What the Google Controversy Misses: The Business Case for Diversity," *The Wall Street Journal*, 13 August 2017, www.wsj.com/articles/what-the-google-controversy-misses-the-business-case-for-diversity-1502625603.

9. "A CEO's Guide to Gender Equality," McKinsey & Company, November 2015, www.mckinsey.com/global-themes/leadership/a-ceos-guide-

to-gender-equality; Jonathan Woetzel, Anu Madgavkar, Kweilin Ellingrud, Eric Labaye, Sandrine Devillard, Eric Kutcher, James Manyika, Richard Dobbs, and Mekala Krishnan, "How Advancing Women's Equality Can Add $12 Trillion to Global Growth," McKinsey Global Institute, September 2015, www.mckinsey.com/ global-themes/employment-and-growth/how-advancing-womens-equality-can-add-12-trillion-to-global-growth.

10. Beth Brooke-Marciniak, Uschi Schreiber, and Karyn Twaronite, "Women. Fast Forward," EY.com, www.ey.com/Publication/ vwLUAssets/ey-women-fast-forward-thought-leadership/$FILE/ey-women-fast-forward-thought-leadership.pdf.

11. Paradigm for Parity, "Inequality in Corporate Leadership," available at www.paradigm4parity. com/problem#the-facts.

12. "Investing in Women: New Evidence for the Business Case," International Finance Corporation, April 2017, www.ifc.org/wps/ wcm/connect/dc30bd0e-392a-4d05-b536-81e3afdd1a25/Investing+in+Women+April+2017A. pdf?MOD=AJPERES.

Chapter 2: The WE 4.0 Framework

1. Klaus Schwab, "The Fourth Industrial Revolution," World Economic Forum, 3 July 2017, www. weforum.org/about/the-fourth-industrial-revolution-by-klaus-schwab.

2. Jeni Klugman, "A Profile of Gender Disparities in the G20: What Is Needed to Close Gaps in the Labor Market," International Economics Department, Chatham House, the Royal Institute of Economic Affairs, November 2015, www. chathamhouse.org/sites/files/chathamhouse/publications/research/20151127GenderG20.pdf.

3. "07 Steps to Conscious Inclusion: A Practical Guide to Accelerating More Women into Leadership," Manpower Group, 7 August 2015, http://manpowergroup. com/wps/wcm/connect/77c2ae4b-e850-44ee-b2b8-6d95e6eab8a5/Seven+Steps+to+Conscious+Inclusion. pdf?MOD=AJPERES.

4. "The Global Gender Gap Report 2017," World Economic Council, 2 November 2017, www3. weforum.org/docs/WEF_GGGR_2017.pdf.

5. Till Leopold and Vesselina Stefanova Ratcheva, "Why It Could Take 1,000 Years for Men and Women to Be Equal in South Asia," World

Economic Forum, 26 October 2016, www.
weforum.org/agenda/2016/10/1000-years-till-
gender-equality-south-asia.

6. Ibid.

7. Elisabeth K. Kelan, "Linchpin – Men, Middle
Managers and Gender Inclusive Leadership,"
Cranfield International Centre for Women
Leaders, Cranfield School of Management,
https://30percentclub.org/assets/uploads/
UK/Third_Party_Reports/Kelan_2014_MIddle_
Managers_and_Gender_inclusion.pdf.

8. Elisabeth K. Kelan, "Men Doing and Undoing
Gender at Work: A Review and Research
Agenda," *International Journal of Management
Reviews*, May 2017, http://onlinelibrary.wiley.com/
wol1/doi/10.1111/ijmr.12146/full.

Chapter 3: Eliminate

1. "Making the Invisible Visible: Gender
Microaggression," UNH Advance, 21 July
2017, www.unh.edu/sites/www.unh.edu/
files/departments/unh_advance/PDFs/
microaggressions.pdf.

2. Jeni Klugman, "A Profile of Gender Disparities
in the G20: What is Needed to Close Gaps in
the Labour Market," International Economics
Department, Chatham House, the Royal Institute

of Economic Affairs, November 2015, www.
chathamhouse.org/sites/files/chathamhouse/
publications/research/20151127GenderG20.pdf.

3. Clémentine Pirlot, "I Almost Left Tech Today,
Here's Why," Code Like a Girl, 27 July 2017,
https://code.likeagirl.io/i-almost-left-tech-today-
heres-why-6d146a2f7cf2.

4. "Women in the Workplace 2016," http://LeanIn.
org and McKinsey & Company, published
September 2016, https://womenintheworkplace.
com.

5. Malin Malmstrom, Jeaneth Johansson,
and Joakim Wincent, "We Recorded VCs'
Conversations and Analyzed How Differently
They Talk about Female Entrepreneurs," *Harvard
Business Review*, 17 May 2017, https://hbr.
org/2017/05/we-recorded-vcs-conversations-
and-analyzed-how-differently-they-talk-about-
female-entrepreneurs.

6. David M. Mayer, "How Not to Advocate for
Women at Work," *Harvard Business Review*, 26
July 2017, https://hbr.org/2017/07/how-not-to-
advocate-for-a-woman-at-work.

7. Kristen Pressner, "Are You Biased? I Am,"
TEDxBasel speech, 30 August 2016, www.
youtube.com/watch?v=Bq_xYSOZrgU.

8. Michael Kimmel, "Getting Men to Speak Up," *Harvard Business Review*, 30 January 2018, https://hbr.org/2018/01/getting-men-to-speak-up.

Chapter 4: Expand

1. "When the Boss is a Woman," American Psychological Association, 26 March 2006, www.apa.org/research/action/boss.aspx.

2. "Women in the Workplace 2016," http://LeanIn.org and McKinsey & Company, September 2016, https://womenintheworkplace.com.

3. Jessica Hill, "Cummins Middle East setting example for appointing more women executives in the GCC," *National*, United Arab Emirates edition, 3 August 2016, www.thenational.ae/business/cummins-middle-east-setting-example-for-appointing-more-women-executives-in-the-gcc-1.146434.

4. Dominic Barton, "It's Time for Companies to Try a New Gender-Equality Playbook," *The Wall Street Journal*, 27 September 2016, www.wsj.com/articles/its-time-for-companies-to-try-a-new-gender-equality-playbook-1474963861.

5. "As Emerging Multinationals Take Off, Are They Leaving Women at the Gate?," Knowledge@Wharton, 25 March 2016,

http://knowledge.wharton.upenn.edu/article/
as-emerging-multinationals-take-off-are-they-
leaving-women-at-the-gate.

6. Richard H. Thaler and Cass Sunstein, *Nudge:
Improving Decisions about Health, Wealth, and
Happiness* (New Haven, CT: Yale University
Press, 2008), pp. 7–8.

7. Kathy Caprino, "The Next Women's Movement
Is Integrating Men: 6 Critical Steps," *Forbes*,
11 September 2014, www.forbes.com/sites/
kathycaprino/2014/09/11/the-next-womens-
movement-is-integrating-men-6-critical-
steps/#49eb17f67906.

8. D. Gaucher, J. Friesen, and A.C. Kay, "Evidence
That Gendered Wording in Job Advertisements
Exists and Sustains Gender Inequality," *Journal
of Personality and Social Psychology* 101, no.
1 (July 2011): 109–128, www.ncbi.nlm.nih.gov/
pubmed/21381851.

9. Stefanie K. Johnson, David R. Hekman, and Elsa
T. Chan, "If There's Only One Woman in Your
Candidate Pool, There's Statistically No Chance
She'll Be Hired," *Harvard Business Review*, 26
April 2016, https://hbr.org/2016/04/if-theres-
only-one-woman-in-your-candidate-pool-theres-
statistically-no-chance-shell-be-hired.

10. Thaler and Sunstein, *Nudge*, p. 3.

11. Tara Sophia Mohr, "Why Women Don't Apply for Jobs Unless They're 100% Qualified," *Harvard Business Review*, 25 August 2014, https://hbr.org/2014/08/why-women-dont-apply-for-jobs-unless-theyre-100-qualified.

12. Shelley Correll and Caroline Simard, "Research: Vague Feedback Is Holding Women Back," *Harvard Business Review*, 29 April 2016, https://hbr.org/2016/04/research-vague-feedback-is-holding-women-back.

13. Iris Bohnet, "Real Fixes for Workplace Bias," *The Wall Street Journal,* 11 March 2016, www.wsj.com/articles/real-fixes-for-workplace-bias-1457713338.

14. David Gelles, "How Nasdaq C.E.O. Adena Friedman Beat the Odds on Wall Street," *New York Times,* 23 March 2018, www.nytimes.com/2018/03/23/business/adena-friedman-nasdaq-corner-office.html.

15. "Women in the Workplace 2016," http://LeanIn.org and McKinsey & Company, September 2016, https://womenintheworkplace.com.

16. Riva Richmond, "Meet the Men Who Invest in Women Entrepreneurs," *The Story Exchange*, 10 August 2017, http://thestoryexchange.org/meet-men-invest-women- entrepreneurs.

17. Gené Teare and Ned Desmond, "The First Comprehensive Study on Women in Venture Capital and Their Impact on Female Founders," *Tech Crunch*, 19 April 2016, https://techcrunch. com/2016/04/19/the-first-comprehensive-study-on-women-in-venture-capital.

18. Dana Kanze, Laura Huang, Mark A. Conley, and E. Tory Higgins, "Male and Female Entrepreneurs Get Asked Different Questions by VCs – and It Affects How Much Funding They Get," *Harvard Business Review*, 27 June 2017, https://hbr. org/2017/06/male-and-female-entrepreneurs-get-asked-different-questions-by-vcs-and-it-affects-how-much-funding-they-get.

19. NaNMalin Malmstrom, NaNJeaneth Johansson, and NaNJoakim Wincent, "We Recorded VCs Conversations and Analyzed How Differently They Talk about Female Entrepreneurs," *Harvard Business Review*, 17 May 2017, https://hbr. org/2017/05/we-recorded-vcs-conversations-and-analyzed-how-differently-they-talk-about-female-entrepreneurs.

20. Jodi Kantor, "#MeToo Called for an Overhaul. Are Workplaces Really Changing?," *New York Times*, 23 March 2018, www.nytimes.com/2018/03/23/us/sexual-harassment-workplace-response.html.

Chapter 5: Encourage

1. Barbara Annis and John Gray, *Work with Me: The 8 Blind Spots Between Men and Women* (New York: Palgrave Macmillan, 2013), p. 5.

2. Katharina Rick, Iván Martén, and Ulrike Von Lonski, "Untapped Reserves: Promoting Gender Balance in Oil and Gas," Boston Consulting Group, 12 July 2017, www.bcg.com/publications/2017/energy-environment-people-organization-untapped-reserves.aspx.

3. Sandrine Devillard, Sandra Sancier-Sultan, and Charlotte Werner. "Moving Mind-sets on Gender Diversity: McKinsey Global Survey Results," McKinsey & Company, January 2014, www.mckinsey.com/business-functions/organization/our-insights/moving-mind-sets-on-gender-diversity-mckinsey-global-survey-results.

4. Nikki Waller and Joanne S. Lublin, "What's Holding Women Back in the Workplace?," *Harvard Business Review*, 20 September 2015, www.wsj.com/articles/whats-holding-women-back-in-the-workplace-1443600242.

5. Stephanie Neal and Audrey Smith, "Are We Underselling the Promise of Women in STEM Leadership Roles?," DDI, 23 July 2017, www.ddiworld.com/challenging-thinking/are-we-

underselling-women-in-stem-leadership-roles#.
WW5FYy9pJMU.linkedin.

6. Adrienne B. Hancock and Benjamin A. Rubin, "Influence of Communication Partner's Gender on Language," *Journal of Language and Social Psychology*, 11 May 2014, http://journals.sagepub. com/doi/abs/10.1177/0261927X14533197.

7. "Atlassian Boosted Its Female Technical Hires By 80% – Here's How," *First Round Review*, 23 July 2017, http://firstround.com/review/atlassian-boosted-its-female-technical-hires-by-80-percent-heres-how.

8. Annis and Gray, *Work with Me*, p. 62.

Chapter 6: Engage

1. "A CEO's Guide to Gender Equality," McKinsey & Company, November 2015, www.mckinsey. com/global-themes/leadership/a-ceos-guide-to-gender-equality.

2. Jennifer Garcia-Alonso, Matt Krentz, Frances Brooks Taplett, Claire Tracey, and Miki Tsusaka, "Getting the Most Diversity from Your Dollars," Boston Consulting Group, 21 June 2017, www. bcg.com/publications/2017/people-organization-behavior-culture-getting-the-most-from-diversity-dollars.aspx.

3. Frank Chung, "Why PepsiCo CEO Asks His Team to 'Leave Loudly'," *The Daily Telegraph*, 12 September 2017, www.dailytelegraph.com.au/ business/work/why-pepsico-ceo-asks-his-team-to-leave-loudly/news-story/5467b3ffff387c3a5dd 79ac3a245c868.

4. Ed Attwood, "Putting Saudi Women First: Glowork's Khalid Alkhudair," *Arabian Business*, 5 June 2015, www.arabianbusiness.com/ putting-saudi-women-first-glowork-s-khalid-alkhudair-595050.html.

5. The website of the Pakistan-based professional recruitment and career advisory company Her Career: www.hercareer.pk.

Resources

If you'd like to learn more, here are a few additional studies, books, and videos that I recommend.

Business Case

Paradigm for Parity
www.paradigm4parity.com/problem#the-facts

Credit Suisse – CS Gender 3000 report
www.prnewswire.com/news-releases/credit -suisse-research-institute-releases-the-cs-gender-3000-the-reward-for-change-report-analyzing -the-impact-of-female-representation-in-board-rooms-and-senior-management-300332558.html

Research

Accelerating Gender Parity in the Fourth Industrial Revolution. *White paper, World Economic Forum,*

*www3.weforum.org/docs/WEF_EGW_White_Paper_
Gender_Parity_4IR.pdf*

**What Research Tells Us about How Women
Are Treated at Work.** Gretchen Gavett,
Harvard Business Review. 27 December 2017,
*https://hbr.org/2017/12/what-research-
tells-us-about-how-women-are-treated-at-
work?autocomplete=true*

***Researchers Find Everyone Has a Bias Blind
Spot: Believing You're Less Biased Than Your
Peers Has Detrimental Consequences.*** Shilo Rea,
Carnegie Mellon University, 8 June 2015,
*www.cmu.edu/news/stories/archives/2015/june/
bias-blind-spot.html*

Men's Views On Gender Diversity in the Workplace.
Todd McBrearty, Slideshare, 20 September 2016,
*www.slideshare.net/ToddMcBrearty/mens-views-
on-gender-diversity-in-the-workplace-092016*

***Moving Mind-sets on Gender Diversity: McKinsey
Global Survey results.*** McKinsey & Company,
*www.mckinsey.com/business-functions/
organization/our-insights/moving-mind-sets-on-
gender-diversity-mckinsey-global-survey-results*

***Men as Allies – Engaging Men to Advance
Women in the Workplace.*** Center for Women
and Business, Bentley University,

www.ceoaction.com/media/1434/bentley-cwb-men-as-allies-research-report-spring-2017.pdf

Women in the Workplace 2017. Alexis Krivkovich, Kelsey Robinson, Irina Starikova, Rachel Valentino, and Lareina Yee, McKinsey & Company, October 2017, *www.mckinsey.com/global-themes/gender-equality/ women-in-the-workplace-2017*

Books

That's What She Said: What Men Need to Know (and Women Need to Tell Them) About Working Together, Joanne Lipman (New York: William Morrow, 2018)

Athena Rising: How and Why Men Should Mentor Women, W. Brad Johnson and David Smith (New York: Routledge, 2018)

Unconscious Bias

Seven Day Bias Cleanse. *www.lookdifferent.org/what-can-i-do/bias-cleanse*

Bias Interrupters Worksheet Women's Leadership Edge, *leadershipinstitute.anl.gov/wp-content/uploads/ sites/46/2016/07/2016-04-11-Bias-Interrupters-Worksheet.pdf*

Flip it to test it technique. Kristen Pressner,
TEDxBasel, 2016,
*www.youtube.com/watch?v=Bq_xYSOZrgU&fea-
ture=youtu.be*

Interrupt Bias in Your Workplace.
http://biasinterrupters.org

Inclusive Leadership

Inclusive Leadership: The View from Six Countries.
Jeanine Prime and Elizabeth R. Salib, Catalyst, 2014,
*www.catalyst.org/knowledge/inclusive-leadership-
view-six-countries*

Quiz – Are you an inclusive leader? Catalyst, 2015,
*www.catalyst.org/knowledge/quiz-are-you-inclusive-
leader*

Becoming a Change Agent

*Engaging Men in Gender Initiatives: What
Change Agents Need to Know.* Jeanine Prime
and Corinne A. Moss-Racusin, Catalyst, 2009,
*www.catalyst.org/system/files/Engaging_Men_In_
Gender_Initiatives_What_Change_Agents_Need_
To_Know.pdf*

Sponsorship

Sponsoring Women: What Men Need to Know.
Ida O. Abbott, J.D. (Lake Zurich, IL: Attorney at
Work, 2014),
_www.attorneyatwork.com/law-practice-books/
careers-books/sponsoring-women-print-edition_

Communities

MARC (Men Advocating Real Change) Catalyst,
http://onthemarc.org/registration

MenEngage Alliance (a global alliance of networks
and nongovernmental organizations that work collectively and individually toward advancing gender
justice, human rights, and social justice),
http://menengage.org

The Good Men Project
https://goodmenproject.com/about

Training

White Men as Full Diversity Partners Learning Lab,
https://wmfdp.com/learning-labs

Unconscious Bias Project,
http://unconsciousbiasproject.org

Tool Kits

Male Advocates and Allies: Promoting Gender Diversity in Technology Workplaces, Catherine Ashcraft, Wendy DuBow, Elizabeth Eger, Sarah Blithe, and Brian Sevier, Workforce NCWIT Alliance and National

Center for Women & Information Technology, 2013, *www.ncwit.org/sites/default/files/resources/ menasadvocatesallies_web.pdf*

GOOD Guys: Overcoming Obstacles to Diversity National Conference of Women's Bar Associations, *https://ncwba.org/programs/good-guys-toolkit*

Toolkit for Companies – Paradigm for Parity, *https://static1.squarespace.com/static/ 57e9765e9f7456c76dc1c1c0/t/59ee6e5bb741 1ccab42cabb1/1508798044105/Paradigm_For_ Parity-Abbreviated+10.5.17_BD.pdf*

TED Talks

Why I am done trying to be "man enough," Justin Baldoni, TEDWomen, 2017, *www.ted.com/talks/justin_baldoni_why_i_m_ done_trying_to_be_man_enough#t-988384*

Want Gender Equality? Let's Get Creative,
Kyl Myers, EDxSaltLake City, 2015,
www.youtube.com/watch?v=12t7PYilNQQ

Wanted: Male Engagement! Jeffery Tobias Halter,
TEDxCentennialParkWomen, 2015,
*www.youtube.com/watch?v=peg1UDexND8&fea-
ture=youtu.be*

A Call to Men, Tony Porter, TEDWomen, 2010,
www.ted.com/talks/tony_porter_a_call_to_men

Index

About the Author

Born and raised in countries where the treatment and roles of women are far from equitable, Rania Habiby Anderson saw from an early age how differently men and women were treated.

Fortunate to have parents who believed that their daughters could be and accomplish anything they wanted, she was provided the great opportunity to attend university and graduate school in the United States.

She had an early successful career at Bank of America in an industry dominated by men. In 1998, she became an executive business coach and has since guided male and female business leaders around the world.

Starting in 2010 and over a four-year period, she researched the habits of women succeeding in emerging economies and wrote *Undeterred: The Six Success Habits of Women in Emerging Economies,* the first career-advice book expressly for women in these markets.

To her knowledge, she has never been discriminated against or denied equal opportunities because of her gender. She has benefited from the sponsorship of male and female business leaders in her corporate and entrepreneurial endeavors. These personal experiences taught her that most men want to, and do, treat women fairly and that success comes from men and women working together. She is fueled by a deeply held belief that the global economy can only thrive when women are equally engaged in driving and leading its prosperity.

Rania is an international speaker, an executive coach, the founder of The Way Women Work (www.TheWayWomenWork.com), the cofounder of a women's angel investor network, and a committed mentor. Her most cherished roles are as wife and mother.